HOLD ON TO HOPE

THE FOOLISHNESS OF GOD

Hold on to Hope

THE FOOLISHNESS OF GOD

Wilfrid J. Harrington OP

DOMINICAN PUBLICATIONS

First published (1998) by
Dominican Publications
42 Parnell Square
Dublin 1

ISBN 1-871552-65-6

British Library Cataloguing in Publications Data.
A catalogue record for this book is available
from the British Library.

Cover design by David Cooke

Printed in Ireland by
The Leinster Leader Ltd, Naas, Co. Kildare

DEDICATION

For E.P.L.

A tree hath hope ...
(Job 14:7)

Contents

Introduction

The occasion of this book, and the burden of its first chapter, is the discovery, in the Old Testament prophetical writings, of a remarkably consistent pattern. It is a pattern of abrupt contrast between divine word of threat and condemnation and word of forgiveness and salvation. Not infrequently – and this is especially so in Second Isaiah – the message of consolation stands by itself, without immediate negative contrast. I argue that, in either case, we have a firm pointer: God's last word is forgiveness and salvation. This is no more than Paul, in his Christian context, had declared: 'God was in Christ reconciling the world to himself' (2 Cor 5:19). Always, salvation is of God alone. And God is loving and faithful. He is Creator, in love with his creation. He is Parent who will not give up on his children, in spite of their ungraciousness.

In our world salvation is still a matter of hope. We may believe that, in principle, salvation has been achieved. Our experience, personal and of our world, constantly reminds us that, in practice, much is unredeemed. Again, one listens to Paul: 'We know that the whole creation has been groaning in labour pains until now; and not only the creation, but we ourselves, who have the first fruits of the Spirit, groan inwardly while we wait for adoption, the redemption of our bodies. For in hope we were saved' (Rom 8:22-24). We live in a world that has more than its measure of pain. Israel did not suffer stoically but cried out to a God who could relieve pain. Here is a lesson we Christians could profitably take to heart. We live in a world of sin: we are sinners among sinners. We need to acknowledge our sinfulness. Again, Israel points the way of candid confession of sin and of total trust in God's boundless mercy. And here, too, a lesson. Those who pray in repentance do not grovel but maintain quiet dignity. Prayer must always be worthy of the God who is addressed and of the people of God who pray.

Sinners have reason for hope, not despair. God is with us in our vale of tears. Indeed, that last word of God – word of loving forgiveness – should be pushed to its logical conclusion: universal salvation. And there is ground for doing so. This ground is by no means only in the strong statement of Paul: 'For God has imprisoned all in disobedience, that he may be merciful to all' (Rom 11:32). A stream of texts suggesting or affirming uiversal salvation runs through the Old Testament and the New. The view is notably present in Revelation. What then of the doctrine of hell? Because of human freedom – the human possibility of ultimately rejecting God – hell remains a possibility. In any event, the answer rests with God, who wills the salvation of all. God does not will damnation.

One looks, then, to God. God is Creator and Saviour. He is the *Deus humanissimus:* not aloof from his creation. His desire finds expression in personified Wisdom: 'rejoicing in his inhabited world and delighting in the human race' (Prov 8:31). God is infinitely gracious – and has consistently suffered human ungraciousness. This is most painful in a reluctance to acknowledge his boundless love – even in resentment at his mercy to sinners. God has absolute respect for human freedom. The ultimate ungraciousness is disrespect of human dignity in his name!

'God proves his love for us in that while we were still sinners Christ died for us' (Rom 5:8). In Jesus of Nazareth the divine has entered into our history. God has become one among us. If Jesus bears the stamp of God's very being, he does so as a human person, like us in all things. Jesus shows us what God is like. Jesus is God's summons to us, God's challenge to us. We can say, truly, that God is love; we have no idea what divine love is in itself. In Jesus we see God's love in action. We learn that God is a God who is with us in our suffering and in our death. We are sure of it because of the suffering and death of Jesus. And we learn that God's gracious love truly has the last word.

1

My Heart Recoils

My heart recoils within me;
my compassion grows warm and tender.
(Hosea 11:8)

We cannot know God through and through. Our *theo*logical speculation may deceive us into imagining that, somehow, we do. It could be argued that our theological portrait of God veils rather than reveals the true God. We do issue warnings on the hazards of God-language – on the need for realising that it is always analogical: that anything we can say of God falls very short of the mark. It seems that we regularly ignore the warnings. We end up with a scientifically neat God who does not recognize himself in our portrait of him.

It may be that our only hope of reflecting anything of God is in the language of poetry. We might hearken to the genial poet-author of Job. He had sketched the might and wonder of the Creator (Job 26:5-13) and then ruefully observed:

Lo, these are but the outskirts of his ways;
and how small a whisper do we hear of him! (26:14).

When one looks closely at the text of the prophetical books one observes a striking and consistent factor. Not alone in the juxtaposition of oracles but, regularly, within an oracle, we find an abrupt change of mood. There is warning and threat, often usually extensive, to a stubborn and unfaithful people. Then, out of the blue, comes word of salvation. There is no logic to it. That is the beauty of it, and the comfort. There can be no logic because salvation is sheerly grace. God is exuberantly illogical. God's word always is forgiveness. It has to be. He, freely, took the risk of creating humans as free beings. He must, consequently, take responsibility and pay the price. His divine generosity in creation must be matched by the divine generosity of his mercy. A prophetic Paul had glimpsed that. When, at the close of Romans 9-11 he had said goodbye to logic, he could declare not only 'All Israel will be saved' but also, 'For God has imprisoned all in disobedience so that he may be merciful to all' (Rom 11:26,32). The prophet Paul is here in the line of the prophets of Israel. And of course, in line with the prophet Jesus.

God and Sin

God's attitude to sin is in question here. In this respect the story of the Flood (Genesis 6-9) is of major theological significance. It dramatizes the destructive nature of sin and the reaction of God to sin. The episode of the 'sons of God and daughters of humans' (Gen 56:1-4) is meant to mark a stage, far beyond that of the man and woman in Genesis 3, in the futile human striving 'to be like God.' What is in question is wholesale corruption – to such a degree as to threaten human existence. God has to do something about the situation. Though his reaction is grief and sorrow, he unleashed the flood waters.

The centre of the story is 'God remembered Noah' (8:1) – when God remembers things happen (see 19:29; 30:32). That is the turning point: from a path of destruction there is a turn to salvation. The story ends in hope and promise: 'I establish my covenant with you, that never again shall all flesh be cut off by the waters of flood, and never again shall there be a flood to destroy the earth' (9:11). Even more noteworthy is the repeated statement in the introduction and conclusion of the story. At the beginning 'every inclination of the thoughts of their hearts was only evil continually' (6:5). At the close, after the promise that there will never be another Flood, the repeated observation is: 'for the inclination of the human heart is evil from youth' (8:21). God has decided to live with humankind's tendency to evil.

Throughout Genesis we are in the presence of myth: an expression of universal truth. The Flood story is paradigm of an ongoing biblical concern. God represents infinite love and mercy and forgiveness. He wills the salvation of all. God would never launch a flood to destroy humankind; he is not in the business of destruction. The Book of Wisdom puts it aptly: 'all existing things are dear to you and you hate nothing that you have created – why else would you have made it?' (12:24). But ... does that mean God is unconcerned with evil and sin? Obviously not. Here our limited understanding faces a daunting problem. How is one to portray the divinely loving forgiveness of God without conveying the false impression that he shrugs off sin as incidental? The beginning of an answer emerges when we understand that sin is not, and cannot be, direct affront to God. Sin does not affect God in himself. Sin hurts God through his creation. Human sin, whatever shape it takes, is betrayal of our humanness. Sin is an affront to God's purpose for his creation. And God, Creator, grieves over sin. As Creator, God will have the last word, as he spoke the first.

The Prophets

It is not by chance that the prophets, all of them, were poets. Why is it that the prophets have achieved and sustained such influence? It is, in large measure, surely, because of the power of their language. The God imaged by them is presented in words that match their poetic insight. In painting divine emotion, they play on the gamut of human emotions. And, with poetic abandon, they can present contradictory pictures of God: a God who will not hesitate to punish sinners; a God who has preferential option for sinners. The biblical God is anything but the immutable, impassible God of our theological tradition. He, along the line of prophetic understanding, is a full-blooded, indeed an earthy God. And, never for a moment, is he any other than God.

People of their day, the prophets took divine causality very seriously. Theirs was the common assessment voiced in Job: 'Shall we receive the good at the hand of God, and not receive the bad?' (2:10). Again, they went along with the doctrine of retribution: God rewards virtue and punishes sin. Since, by and large, the prophets had to contend with national disasters – or the threat of them – it was natural for them to view such disasters not only as due to the sinfulness of the people but, also, as divine punishment of sin. It is not surprising that oracles of woe predominate. It is an aspect of their keen pastoral concern.

Like anthropomorphism, the attribution of human features and behaviour to God, anthropathism (the attribution of human feelings to God) is common in biblical language. In short, the Old Testament never speaks of Yahweh without attributing human traits to him. Anthropopathism must point to the *pathos* of God. The Greek word refers to what one has experienced; it surely includes experience of suffering. If we are to be true to the whole biblical picture we shall need to pay far more attention than we have had to the metaphors which point to the suffering of God.[1]

Neglect of them has contributed, in its measure, to the dominant image of God as a dominating Being. Neglect of them has caused many to turn away, in disgust, from a God who seems to display disdainful unconcern for human suffering. Most importantly, these metaphors of pathos are essential ingredients of a balanced portrait of God. They add, immeasurably, to his attractiveness and counter, effectively, many false gods of our religious heritage.

There is, surely, something compelling about a God who grieves for humankind gone astray. A God who suffers because of his people's rejection of him, who suffers with his suffering people, who suffers on behalf of the people, is,

---

1. T.E. Fretheim, *The Suffering God* (Philadelphia: Fortress, 1984); W. Harrington, *The Tears of God* (Collegeville: Liturgical Press, 1992).

indeed, a challenging God. He is, surely, the foolish God discerned by Paul. He is the God who has shown that he is a God not aloof from pain and sorrow and death. He is the God of humankind. He is the *kind* of God we need. He is *our* God.[2]

Our traditional ideas of God may cause us to be somewhat upset by biblical language. It is all very well to hear of the 'love' of God. What of God's 'anger'? In the first place, it is needful to observe again that human language is incapable of enunciating the ineffable reality of God. It, however, remains our only tool. Biblical language reminds us that God is not some vague 'force'; God is personal. The language reflects a vitally important perception. The prophets, and biblical writers, were conscious of the transcendence of Yahweh. They were intensely aware that he was a God close at hand, a God with whom they could and did have dialogue. In speaking of him, and to him, they were prepared to take what we might term 'risk'.

A striking case in point is Hosea. He was the first to represent the covenant relationship of Yahweh with his people as a marriage. It would have seemed natural enough that the covenant between God and Israel might have been likened to the marriage contract. In practice, it is not the contract aspect that is exploited but, instead, the love aspect and, especially, the love of a husband for his wife. Hosea harked back to the wilderness and the entry into the land. He looked to the graciousness of Yahweh and the rank ingratitude of Israel (Hos 9:10; 11:1-12; 13:4-6). Doubtless, Hosea idealized the wilderness years and painted them as the honeymoon period of God and his people. What matters is that he did not hesitate to cast Yahweh as Spouse of Israel. Bold imagery indeed when the Canaanite religion of Baal was the great challenge: the fertility cult of Baal and his consort Astarte. The prophet knew that, despite the risk of

2. See W. Harrington, *Op. cit.*, 26-37.

confusion, what mattered was to proclaim the love of God. Theological prudence would not deter him from flaunting his profound conviction. Some might misunderstand – too bad. But those who, like himself, had known the joy and pain of love would recognize in his long-suffering Spouse their one, true God.

It is plain that the prophets who had, pastorally, to face intransigence from political and religious leaders, and from their own people, retained an insight into divine mercy. Beyond their warnings there is ever a prophetical perception of the profligacy of God. He just will not be confined. His last word simply has to be word of forgiveness.

Amos is the exception that proves the rule. He is a prophet of unrelieved gloom. On the other hand, the present shape of the book of Amos firmly sustains our argument. The final editor felt compelled to provide a thoroughly optimistic conclusion. Nothing up to Amos 9:10 would lead us to expect 9:11-15.

> On that day I will raise up the booth of David that is
>   fallen…
> I will restore the fortunes of my people Israel …
> I will plant them upon their land,
> and they shall never again be plucked up
> out of the land that I have given them,
> says the Lord your God (9:11,14,15).

There is no human logic: the oracle is wholly out of tune. Instead there is divine logic. It is dramatic expression of God's final word – word of salvation. The prophets bear abundant witness to divine illogicality.

HOSEA

The prophet Hosea bears startling witness. Nothing makes any sense – except the crazy sense of an illogical God.

Hosea 2:1-23 [2:3-25 – Hebrew]. **Therefore …**

Plead with your mother, plead –
for she is not my wife, and I am not her husband – …
Therefore I will hedge up her way with thorns;
and I will build a wall against her,
so that she cannot find her paths …
Therefore I will take back my grain in its time …
I will punish her for the festival days of the Baals,
when she offered incense to them …
and went after her lovers,
and forgot me, says the Lord (2:2,6,9,13).

In verses 6 and 9 the 'therefore' (*laken*) introduces, as generally in prophetic texts, a threat (see Amos 3:2; Micah 3:12; Hosea 4:3). The next 'therefore' (v. 14) strikes a startlingly different note.

Therefore, I will now allure her,
and bring her into the wilderness,
and speak tenderly to her …
There she shall respond as in the days of her youth,
as at the time when she came out of the land of Egypt …
And I will take you for my wife forever; I will take you for
  my wife in righteousness and in justice, in steadfast
  love and in mercy. I will take you for my wife in
  faithfulness; and you shall know the Lord (2:14-15,19-
  20).

In v. 14 'the "therefore" of intense judgment has been transposed into an act of protection and solidarity … The voice of harsh threat has inexplicably become the sound of *assurance*'.[3]

In sorrow, Yahweh had divorced his spouse: 'she is not my wife, and I am not her husband'. Here, as a Babel where

---

3. W. Brueggemann, *Hopeful Imagination: Prophetic Voices in Exile* (Philadelphia: Fortress, 1986), 38.

his will to scatter humankind out of his sight (Gen 11:1-9) faltered on his call of Abraham to a new beginning (12:1-3), and as the Flood when his grim decision: 'I will blot out from the earth the human beings I have created ... for I am sorry that I have made them' flows directly into the declaration: 'But Noah found favour in the sight of the Lord' (6:7-8), God is inconsistent. Ever, God's weak side is his love. Divorced Israel may be: the price of unfaithfulness. In God's eyes Israel is still his spouse and he will not give her up.

Hosea 11:1-9. How Can I Give You Up?

When Israel was a child, I loved him,
and out of Egypt I called my son.
The more I called them, the more they went from me ...
Yet it was I who taught Ephraim to walk,
I took them up in my arms;
but they did not know that I healed them.
I led them with cords of human kindness, with bands of
    love.
I was to them like those who lift infants to their cheeks.
I bent down to them and fed them.
They shall return to the land of Egypt,
and Assyria will be their king,
because they have refused to return to me ...
How can I give you up, Ephraim?
How can I hand you over, O Israel? ...
My heart recoils within me;
my compassion grows warm and tender.
I will not execute my fierce anger;
I will not again destroy Ephraim;
for I am God and no mortal,
the Holy One in your midst,
and I will not come in wrath (11:1-5, 8-9).

As in chapter 2 Hosea did not hesitate to present God as Spouse of his people so, now, he daringly pictures him as doting father (arguably, as mother) of a first-born son. As with marital love (chapter 2), parental love, too, meets with ingratitude (11:3-4). The poem had begun on a sad note: 'The more I called them, the more they went from me' (v. 2). They deserve to be sent back to Egypt again (v. 5). God would leave them where he had found them. And he would – but for his vulnerable love (vv. 8-9).

For I am God and no mortal. Taken out of context (as it often is) it might be an assertion of God's transcendence. For Hosea it is a declaration of God's love. Where human love would say 'Enough', God will never set limits. Paradoxically, 'I am God and no mortal' expresses the 'human-ness' of God. It asserts that God is more 'human' than humankind – the *Deus humanissimus*. It is not by chance that the Son of God, come at last to show humankind what being human means, will set nothing else than love as the mark of true humanness.

There is a further point. I have followed the generally accepted exegetical course of taking the image of Hosea 11 to reflect the father-love of God. In fact, a case can be made, and has been made, for an understanding of the passage as imaging God's mother-love.[4] One may, in the first place, observe that the picking up of an infant and a bending down to feed (vv. 3-4) is a vivid description of a mother breast-feeding an infant – all the more indeed when the phrase 'lifting to the cheeks' may be rendered 'lifting to the breasts.'

More thought-provoking is v. 9: 'I am God and no mortal' – 'mortal' (lit. 'man') is not *adam* ('humanity') but *ish*: specifically male. Yahweh is rejecting male behaviour. She is not going to act with stern anger and destroy her people; strong maternal emotions resist such conduct on her part. In chapter 11, then, Yahweh as mother is a warm image of God for Hosea. The mother-love of God shines through the father-

---

4. See Helen Schungel-Straumann, 'Gott als Mutter in Hosea 11,' *Theologische Quartalschrift* 166:2 (1986), 119-34.

love of a prophet. What is undoubted, in either interpretation, is the prophet's stress on God's measureless love.

One can observe a fluctuation throughout Hosea. Chapter 2 has the startling clash of 'therefores' and the assertion of God's tireless love. Then chapters 4-10 are a collection of strongly negative oracles. We have noted the powerful message of chapter 11. Yet, chapter 12 goes on to tell of Israel's perfidy. The book closes with the now familiar contrast.

Hosea 13:12-16; 14:1-8. **I Will love Them Freely.**

Ephraim's iniquity is bound up; his sin is kept in store ...
Shall I ransom them from the power of Sheol?
Shall I redeem them from Death?
O Death, where are your plagues?
O Sheol, where is your destruction?
Compassion is hidden from my eyes (13:12,14).

Yet again, it seems that there is no hope for Ephraim; the time of compassion has run out. Not so. Judgment is not the final word. That final word is word of healing. It is word, not of a Judge but of a Physician.

Return, O Israel, to the Lord your God,
for you have stumbled because of your iniquity ...
I will heal their disloyalty;
I will love them freely,
for my anger has turned from them.
I will be like the dew to Israel ...
O Ephraim, what have I to do with idols?
It is I who answer and look after you.
I am like an evergreen cypress;
your faithfulness comes from me. (14:1, 4-5, 8).

JEREMIAH

'The Book of Jeremiah as it now stands makes a statement about the juxtaposition of judgment and deliverance.'[5] The truth of this observation can be readily documented. In the famous contest between Jeremiah and Hananiah (Jer 28), the former emphatically asserted his conviction of the inevitable invasion and conquest of Nebuchadnezzar (28:13-14). Then, directly, follows Jeremiah's letter to the exiles of the first deportation to Babylon in 597 B.C. (Jer 29:4-14). They were urged to settle down in Babylon and were warned against prophets (like Hananiah) who did not speak in the name of the Lord (29:8-9). Jeremiah offered steadfast hope, but called for patience:

> Thus says the Lord: Only when Babylon's seventy years are completed will I visit you, and I will fulfil to you my promise and bring you back to this place. For surely I know the plans I have for you, says the Lord, plans for your welfare and not for harm, to give you a future with hope (29:10-11).

National disaster was unavoidable. Yet, Jeremiah can assure these early exiles that their God had promised a restoration.

A regular assessment of Jeremiah, reflected in the term 'jeremiad', is not really true to the prophet. Certainly, the Jeremiah of the book emerges, in the last analysis, as prophet of hope. The vocational passage (1:4-10) had specified that the message of the prophet would involve not only plucking up and destruction but also building and planting (1:10). The texts of 'building and planting' are concentrated in chapters 29-33. These chapters all concern hope. The poetic centre is chapters 30-31. And here we find the contrast:

> For thus says the Lord: your hurt is incurable, your wound is grievous. There is no medicine for your wound, no

5. W. Brueggemann, *Op. cit.,* 11.

healing for you ... Because your guilt is great, because your sins are so numerous, I have done these things to you (30:12-13, 15).

The ring of finality seems to exclude all hope. Then, abruptly, is the assurance:

Therefore all who devour you shall be devoured ...
I will restore health to you, and your wounds I will heal, says the Lord (v. 17).

It is noteworthy that the transitional verse 16 opens with 'therefore.' We have noted above the significance of the word.

Jer 32:26-44 The Fate of Jerusalem

In 32:26-35 the word of the Lord to Jeremiah tells of his decision to surrender Jerusalem to Nebuchadnezzar because of the appalling sinfulness of the people. This is wholly consonant with the burden of the prophet's message. Suddenly, in vv. 36-44, is a promise of restoration: 'They shall be my people, and I will be their God ... I will make an everlasting covenant with them' (vv. 38, 40). No reason is offered for the radical turnabout; it is, solely, God's sovereign decision. 'For thus says the Lord: Just as I have brought all this disaster upon this people, so I will bring upon them all the good fortune that I now promise them' (v. 42). Perhaps, after all, the reason is given: 'I will rejoice in doing good to them' (v. 41). The reason is God himself: his last word is always forgiveness.

EZEKIEL

Walter Brueggemann speaks of Ezekiel's 'two-stage theology.' The first stage is the work of judgment; the second stage is the work of life.[6] Here, again, is that contrast we have been stressing. We look to the more striking passages.

6. *Op. cit.,* 72.

Ezekiel 11:5-20. **Oracle Against Jerusalem**

The prophet, now exiled to Babylon, has a vision of leaders of the people at the temple: 'These are the men who devise iniquity and who give wicked counsel in this city … therefore prophesy against them' (11:2,34). The prophet pronounced his oracle against the leaders (11:5-12). 'I will bring the sword upon you … I will judge you at the border of Israel. Then you shall know that I am the Lord' (1:8, 11-12). In v. 13 there is his pained protestation: 'Ah, Lord God! will you make a full end of the remnant of Israel?' Then, the Lord's immediate response (11:14-20) is a word of firm promise:

> Thus says the Lord God: I will gather you from the peoples, and assemble you out of the countries where you have been scattered, and I will give you the land of Israel … I will give them one heart, and put a new spirit within them; I will remove the heart of stone from their flesh and give them a heart of flesh … Then they shall be my people, and I will be their God (11:17-20).

16:1-63 **Jerusalem the Unfaithful**

Ezekiel 16:1-52 is the lengthy, and consciously crude, allegory of the 'brazen whore' Jerusalem. One must candidly acknowledge that the imagery and language are offensive to women. This is a salutary reminder not only that the Bible is an androcentric text but that, until very recently, the whole of theology was firmly male-centred. Granted this, the Ezekiel text is important. Jerusalem had acted more abominably than her sisters Samaria and Sodom: 'So be ashamed and bear your disgrace, for you have made your sisters appear righteous' (v. 52). Then, with startling abruptness, comes v. 53 - 'I will restore their fortunes, the fortunes of Sodom and her daughters, and I will restore your own fortunes along with theirs.' The passage 16:53-63 is an oracle of restoration:

> I will remember my covenant with you in the days of your youth and I will establish with you an everlasting cov-

enant ... I will establish my covenant with you, and you shall know that I am the Lord ... when I forgive you all that you have done, says the Lord God (vv. 60, 62-63).

33:10-11 **Restoration**

Ezekiel 33-39 is, in the main, a collection of oracles of restoration. The three verses 33:10-11 sound the keynote:

> Now you, mortal, say to the house of Israel, Thus you have said: 'Our transgressions and our sins weigh upon us, and we waste away because of them; how then can we live?' Say to them, As I live says the Lord God, I have no pleasure in the death of the wicked, but that the wicked turn from their ways and live; turn back, turn back, from your evil ways; for why will you die, O house of Israel?

The sinfulness of Israel is manifest and acknowledged. Against it is the generous invitation to return to life. Death (separation from God) is not the desire of God. He seeks not death but life – loving union with him.

37:1-14 **The Valley of Bones**

This powerful vision was inspired by the people's complaint in v. 11: 'Our bones are dried up' The passage opens with a vision of a battlefield littered with the dried-out, scattered bones of the slain. Ezekiel is asked: 'Mortal, can these bones live?' Wisely, he answered: 'O Lord God, you know' (v. 3). It is not just a matter of human prudence; already we are being pointed to divine initiative. Through the power of the word and spirit of the Lord there came a radical transformation. 'I prophesied as he commanded me, and the breath (spirit) came into them, and they lived, and stood on their feet, a vast multitude' (v. 10). Very like a passage in Isaiah (Isa 5-7), the meaning of the parabolic vision is spelled out:

> Then he said to me, 'Mortal, these bones are the whole house of Israel. They say, "Our bones are dried up, and

our hope is lost; we are cut off completely." Therefore, prophesy and say to them, Thus says the Lord God: I am going to open your graves, and bring you up from your graves, O my people; and I will bring you back to the land of Israel. And you shall know that I am the Lord, when I open your graves, and bring you up from your graves, O my people. I will put my spirit within you, and you shall live, and I will place you on your own soil; then you shall know that I, the Lord, have spoken and will act,' says the Lord (37:11-14).

In the three historical reviews (chapters 16; 20; 23) Ezekiel seemed to wish to say all that could be said about Israel's unfaithfulness, its indifference to the love of God, and its utter failure to obey. The picture he painted could scarcely be blacker than it is. But we need to keep in mind that he, in keeping with his theology, was justifying the divine chastisement which must fall in the near future: even divine patience had at last run out.

We need also to observe that the prophet pointed to God's saving will – now more than ever seen to be free and unmerited (see 16:60-63; 20:40-44). In this sense, the three sombre chapters are the prelude to the glory of Yahweh's deed, for it is evident that his salvation cannot be based on any worth in Israel itself. Paul will follow much the same technique when, on a broader canvas, he will paint, in black, the sinful helplessness of humankind, as a backdrop to God's incredibly gracious saving deed in Christ (Rom 1-8).

ISAIAH

A first matter to be cleared up is the complex structure of the Book of Isaiah and its broad chronological sweep. The acknowledged scholarly view is that Isaiah falls into three parts: Isaiah 1-39 which contains oracles of the eight-century prophet, Isaiah ben-Amoz; Isaiah 40-55, known as Second Isaiah; and Isaiah 56-66, often referred to as Third Isaiah. The background of Second Isaiah is the close of the Babylonian captivity, while Third Isaiah is set in Judah in the early days of the return. So far so good. But there is the complicating factor that, in chapters 1-39, only chapters 1-12 and 28-33 give, in the main, the words of Isaiah ben-Amoz – the rest is largely post-exilic. Our interest, here, is the present form of the book of Isaiah – which may be called its canonical shape. And our concern is to discern the juxtaposition of threat and promise.

Isaiah 30:1-26 Waiting for Yahweh

In Isaiah 30:1-17 there is a severe indictment:

> Oh, rebellious children, says the Lord,
> who carry out a plan, but not mine ...
> For they are a rebellious people, faithless children,
> children who will not hear the instruction of the Lord ...
> For thus said the Lord God, the Holy One of Israel:
> in returning and rest you shall be saved;
> in quietness and in trust shall be your strength.
> But you refused and said, 'No!' (vv. 1,9,15-16).

Then, at v. 18, an abrupt change of tone:

> Therefore the Lord waits to be gracious to you;
> therefore he will rise up to show mercy to you.

And vv. 19-17 spell out the blessedness to come. Notable are the truly beautiful verses:

> Though the Lord may give you the bread of adversity and the water of affliction, yet your Teacher will not hide himself any more, but your eyes shall see your Teacher. And when you turn to the right or when you turn to the left, your ears shall hear a word behind you, saying, 'This is the way; walk in it' (vv. 20-21).

40:1-11 **Call to Return**

The opening passage (Isa 40:1-11) strikes the note of the Book of Consolation (Isa 40-55). The exuberant language serves a purpose. It is evident that, among the exiles, there was little yearning for a return. This was, predominantly, a second generation, doing quite nicely in Babylon. A devastated and impoverished homeland of their fathers did not beckon compellingly. The prophet has to drum up some enthusiasm. While, humanly speaking, there were no grounds for optimism, he can assure his people that God is ready once again to bring them out of captivity and into the promised land. This time Yahweh will lead them in solemn procession along a Via Sacra, a processional way hewn through mountain, valley and desert, all the long way from Babylon to Jerusalem. This time there will be no years of wandering. God will manifest his glory (40:3) through his saving deed on behalf of his people. He is the constant God, unlike the ephemeral grass-like nature of humanity (vv. 6-8). His 'word' stands forever: 'For the mountains may depart and the hills be removed, but my steadfast love shall not depart from you, and my covenant of peace shall not be removed, says the Lord, who has compassion on you' (54:10).

43: 22-25 **Yahweh Alone Saves**

You did not call upon me, O Jacob;
but you have been weary of me, O Israel! ...
I have not burdened you with offerings,
or wearied you with frankincense ...
But you have burdened me with your sins;
you have wearied me with your iniquities (vv. 22,23,24).

God had chosen Israel as his own and had made a covenant with his people. Now, he suffers when he is spurned and rejected by his people. He suffers because he is, and will be, faithful. God is never one who stands calmly aloof, impervious to being spurned and rejected. He is one who grieves over a broken relationship – grieves for the tragic unfaithful partner. God treats the human partner in the relationship with total seriousness and scrupulously respects human freedom. His patience is inexhaustible; he cannot be worn down. He is determined to restore the relationship. This is why we have, out of the blue, v. 25:

I, I am He
who blots out your transgressions for my own sake,
and I will not remember your sins.

Again: the last word is forgiveness.

49:14-18 Consolation

But Zion said, 'The Lord has forsaken me,
my Lord has forgotten me.'
Can a woman forget her nursing child.
or show no compassion for the child of her womb?
Even these may forget,
yet I will never forget you.
See, I have inscribed you on the palms of my hands (vv. 14-
16).

The human cry of Godforsakenness is answered by words of most tender assurance. One is reminded of another cry of Godforsakenness – answered by the new life of resurrection (see Mark 15:34-39).

51:17-23 I Will Comfort You

Stand up, O Jerusalem,
you have drunk at the hand of the Lord
the cup of his wrath ...
These two things have befallen you
– who will grieve with you –
devastation and destruction, famine and sword
– who will comfort you? ...
Thus says your Sovereign, the Lord,

your God who pleads the cause of his people:
see, I have taken from your hand the cup of staggering;
you shall drink no more from the bowl of my wrath (vv.
17,19,22).

On the one hand, God's people had been given to drink of the bowl of his wrath. This same Sovereign Lord is he who pleads the cause of his people; there will be no more 'wrath.' This is remarkably like the Genesis flood story – see Gen 6:5-7;8:21-22. Perhaps, even more, is it like Romans 8:31-39.

54:4-10 The Faithful Spouse
This stirringly beautiful passage goes to the heart of the matter. Here we see, with clarity, *why* God's final word is mercy: it is because it cannot be other. He is this kind of God.

Do not fear, for you will not be ashamed …
For your Maker is your husband,
the Lord of hosts is his name;
the Holy One of Israel is your Redeemer,
the God of the whole earth he is called.
For the Lord has called you
like a wife forsaken and grieved in spirit,
like the wife of a man's youth when she is cast off,
says your God.
For a brief moment I abandoned you,
but with great compassion I will gather you.
In overflowing wrath for a moment I hid my face from
you,
but with everlasting love I will have compassion on
you,
says the Lord, your Redeemer.

This is like the days of Noah to me:
Just as I swore that the waters of Noah
would never again go over the earth,
so I have sworn that I will not be angry with you

and I will not rebuke you.
For the mountains may depart and the hills be removed,
but my steadfast love shall not depart from you,
and my covenant of love shall not be removed,
says the Lord, who has compassion on you (54:4-10).

Hosea 1-3 and the Flood-story (Gen 6-9) stand behind this passage. Israel, unfaithful wife, had been divorced; now her faithful Spouse welcomes her back. He can do no other. His 'wrath' is momentary; his compassion is as firm as his everlasting love. God recalls his promise to Noah and re-phrases it, in stronger terms, in favour of Israel. An unshakable covenant of peace is based on his steadfast love. He is Lord of com-passion: a God who suffers with his suffering children. God does suffer because of his people's rejection of him. God suffers for the people.

62:1-5 **Splendid Impatience**

'For a long time I have held my peace' (Isa 42:14). God can no longer hold his breath.

You shall no more be termed Forsaken.
and your land shall no longer be termed Desolate;
but you shall be called My Delight in Her,
and your land Married;
for the Lord delights in you,
and your land shall be married.
For as a young man marries a young woman,
so shall your builder marry you,
and as the bridegroom rejoices over the bride,
so shall your God rejoice over you (62:4-5).

Again, the manifest influence of Hosea, and again the image of the eternally faithful Spouse/Mother – 'How can I give you up, O Israel!'

65:1-25 **Here I Am**

I was ready to be sought by those who did not ask,
to be found by those who did not seek me.
I said, 'Here I am, here I am,'
to a nation that did not call on my name.
I held out my hands all day long
to a rebellious people ...
I will not keep silent, but I will repay;
I will indeed repay into their laps
their iniquities and their ancestors' iniquities together,
says the Lord ...
For I am about to create new heavens and a new earth;
the former things shall not be remembered or come to
    mind.
But be glad and rejoice forever in what I am creating;
for I am about to create Jerusalem as a joy,
and its people as a delight.
I will rejoice in Jerusalem,
and delight in my people (vv. 1-2,6-7,17-19).

God calls out, repeatedly – but in vain. There is threat of his 'wrath.' Instead, he will bring about a new creation. His renewed people will be his pride and joy.

1:2-3; 66:10-13 **Beginning and End**

The opening and the close of canonical Isaiah aptly illustrate the contrast of threat and salvation.

Hear, O heavens, and listen, O earth;
for the Lord has spoken:
I reared children and brought them up,
but they have rebelled against me.
The ox knows its master's crib;
but Israel does not know,
my people do not understand (1:2-3)

The Book opens on this note of bewilderment, God is a parent, cut to the quick by the ingratitude of children. That sad ingratitude is documented in chapter after chaper of Isaiah. Nevertheless we have, in the meantime, been so well prepared that we have come to take for granted the tone of the closing chapter.

> Rejoice with Jerusalem, and be glad for her,
> all you who love her;
> rejoice with her in joy,
> all you who mourn over her –
> that you may nurse and be satisfied
> from her consoling breasts;
> that you may drink deeply with delight
> from her glorious bosom.
> For thus says the Lord:
> I will extend prosperity to her like a river,
> and the wealth of the nations like an overflowing stream;
> and you shall nurse and be carried on her arm,
> and dandled on her knees.
> As a mother comforts her child,
> so I will comfort you;
> you shall be comforted in Jerusalem (66:10-13).

Here, God's children nurse at the breast of Jerusalem – a lovely image of peace and contentment. Striking is the switch in v. 13 to the motherhood of God. In Ezekiel 34 God had had enough of alleged shepherds; he decided to take personal charge. We get a similar picture here with God becoming a nursing mother. And we are back, again, to Hosea, chapter 11.

Divine Vulnerability
What has been offered above is a very confined cross-section, no more than that. The remarkable fluctuation we have noted in the prophets can be documented over and

over again. It is not rarity; it is the norm.[7] This must surely tell us something of our God. And this feature is to be found not only in the prophets. The God of the Bible, the Father of our Lord Jesus Christ, is the foolish God. (see Corinthians 1:18-21). His gamble was in making us free. He stands, stolidly, by that gamble. God is, happily, not an Unmoved Mover. He is not even Creator. He is PARENT. And just there is his divine vulnerability. What loving parent can ever, ever, reject the child? Our human grace is not that we are creatures of God, not even that we are image of God. The ultimate divine foolishness, made public in Christian revelation, is that we are *children* of God. That is Christian truth – but it must reach into all of humankind.

7. See *Appendix*, pp. 83-86, *infra*.

2

Response

Therefore I will not restrain my mouth;
I will speak in the anguish of my spirit;
I will complain in the bitterness of my soul
(Job 7:11)

The Bible is dialogue of God and humankind. Our first chapter has looked at aspects of God's contribution. This chapter looks to aspects of the human response. It is response in prayer: prayer of lament and prayer of repentance.

Lament
Lament is, for all practical purpose, not part of Christian worship. And that is a pity. Laments pervade the Old Testament (and they are not absent from the New). Lament in the Psalter marks only a portion of the whole. Lament is rooted in the fact that the human of whom the Old Testament speaks is finite. The Old Testament knows of humankind only within the limitations of the creation story of Genesis 1-3. Creation faith accepts that God willed to create the world as it is and humans as they are. It accepts, without remainder, that finitude – contingency – is an inevitable feature of created reality. We are conscious of struggle in our world; we experience struggle within ourselves. The finitude of our world is caught up in God's world of creation. The peril created by these limitations is part and parcel of human existence. It is human destiny to be human beings in a world of failure and suffering. We need to come to terms with suffering as a factor of our experience – of life itself. Here is where lament comes in.

As not a few would see it, lament cannot be prayer; it can

have no place in prayer. Suffering is to be borne – one 'offers it up;' it is not to be lamented. This is not the view of the Bible. There, lamentation reflects the reality of human existence. If pain and suffering are characteristic of human existence (see Genesis 3), the expressing of pain is intrinsic to human life (see Mark 14:34-36; 15:34 – Gethsemane and the cry on the cross). Lamentation is the language of suffering. Lament is addressed to God, because God is the One who can take away suffering.[1]

The language of lament can be uninhibited in face of suffering that can no longer be comprehended. The accusation is mounted: How could God have allowed this to happen? The accusation is made in the context of talking with God, the context of prayer. It is the very relationship with God that makes the complaint possible. Think of the Cross: My God, my God, why have you forsaken me? It is not at all surprising that lamentation figures so largely in the Psalter. Indeed, praise and lament dominate – and the lament is quite as fully prayer as is the praise.

Jesus' cry on the cross (Mk 15:34) is obviously a lament. But so was his word over Jerusalem:

> As he came near Jerusalem and saw the city, he wept over it, saying, 'If you, even you, had only recognized on this day the things that made for peace! But now they are hidden from your eyes. (Lk 19: 41-42).

Jesus lamented over the suffering that the destruction of Jerusalem by the Romans will bring upon the city's inhabit-

---

1. 'That sufferers have been given the opportunity to pour out their hearts before God, precisely in the language of the lament, is seen in the Old Testament as itself an expression of divine mercy. Modern psychotherapy has long recognized that lamentation can have healing power, that openly expressing the pain of suffering can ameliorate its impact upon the sufferer. In the Bible, then, the liberating possibility is opened up for sufferers to bewail their suffering directly to God. In the Bible, sufferers are allowed to voice their lament directly to their Lord.' C.Westermann, *Lamentations. Issues and Interpretation* (Edinburgh: T & T Clark,1994), p. 91.

ants. He directed his compassion to a surfeit of suffering, in particular, suffering of the innocent. He anticipated the lamentation of the sufferers.[2]

LAMENT FOR THE DEAD

There are two kinds of lament: lament for the dead and lament of affliction. Lament for the dead looks backward and bewails the death of another. A striking example is David's lament for the slain Saul and Jonathan (2 Sam 1:19-27). It is quite like the Irish *caoine*. The lament of affliction (our interest here) looks forward: the sufferer, lamenting what has happened to oneself, reaches out for life and begs that the suffering be taken away. The lament is not preoccupation with one's sufferings (though they may be graphically chronicled); it is not self-pity. It is concerned with removal of suffering; it is an appeal to the One who can take away suffering. A lament regularly turns into praise – an anticipation of being saved. The praise conclusion is an expression of trust and hope: trust in a compassionate God and the hope that compassion will lead to the assuaging of suffering.

When it comes to Old Testament prayer many think exclusively of the Psalter. The truth is: prayer, and of course lament, pervades the Old Testament. The cry of distress (and hence the lament) goes back to the narrative of deliverance from Egypt:

> The Israelites groaned under their slavery and cried out. Out of the slavery their cry for help rose up to God. God heard their groaning, and God remembered his covenant

---

2.   'When Jesus weeps over Jerusalem, he anticipates the lamentation of those who will have to face the horrors of the conquest of Jerusalem in the year 70 A.D. Not only that, but he shares in their suffering! By proleptically sharing in the impending lamentation over Jerusalem, Jesus also retroactivally gives to the laments which were raised on the occasion of the city's earlier destruction [587 B.C.] their dignity as a proper response to suffering.' C. Westermann, Op. cit., 232.

with Abraham, Isaac, and Jacob. God looked upon the
Israelites, and God took notice of them (Ex 2:23-25).

There are the bones of lament: the cry of deliverance and,
implicitly, the praise that would follow on God's 'remembering.'

LAMENT OF AFFLICTION

There are two kinds of lament of affliction: lament of the
people – communal lament – and lament of the individual.
With Job we will concentrate on the individual lament. A
glance, however, at the communal lament will introduce us
to the bold address of Israel to its God. Two questions recur
in communal lament: 'Why?' and 'How long?' The question
'Why?' asks why God had rejected, abandoned or forgotten
his people. The question 'How long?' implies an enduring
distress and expresses impatience at the duration. The point
is that the accusatory questions are directed at God. Psalm 44
is a splendid illustration.

In this communal lament Israel ponders on the seeming
absence of the God of Israel. It opens with a recital of God's
interventions on behalf of the ancestors: 'our ancestors have
told us what deeds you performed in their days, in the days
of old' (44:1-3). The victories of the Israelites were won by
Yahweh's exploits on their behalf. Now, inexplicably, God
has turned against his people: 'You have rejected us ... You
have made us turn back from the foe ... You have sold your
people for a trifle ... You have made us a byword among the
nations' (44:9-16). The signs of God's dereliction of duty are
glaring. To add insult to injury, he did not even demand a
decent price for his property.[3]

Israel protests that it has not deserved such treatment:

All this has come upon us, yet we have not forgotten you,

3. See J.F. Craghan, *The Psalms* (Wilmington, DE: M. Glazier, 1985), pp.
140-145.

> or been false to your covenant.
> Our heart has not turned back,
> nor have our steps departed from your way (vv. 17-18).

Worst of all, their God is responsible for the calamity:

> Because of you we are being killed all day long,
> and accounted as sheep for the slaughter (v. 22)

This only sums up the emphasis throughout vv. 9-16: God has to answer for the sorry situation. Then comes the bold challenge of vv. 23-26:

> Rouse yourself! Why do you sleep, O Lord?
> Why do you hide your face?

This is no time for God to sleep. It is high time he became conspicuous by his presence, not his absence. It is high time he remembered his covenant with his people. The psalm closes on this hope:

> Rise up, come to our help.
> Redeem us for the sake of your steadfast love (v. 26).

There is robust prayer indeed. And it is only one instance. By itself it emphatically confounds a widespread delusion that the God of the Old Testament is a God who inspired fear – even dread. Instead, Israel had a refreshingly direct approach to its God – perhaps nowhere more than in prayer. While it is true that most of the communal psalms do acknowledge the people's sin, always the ultimate hope is in Yahweh's covenant faithfulness.

Job

The Book of Job offers the highpoint of lament. Its hero, Job, is an outstanding witness of challenge with his harrowing journey from faith to faith. It was an epic journey, though he had not stirred from his seat among the ashes. He groped through a dark night, throwing down the gauntlet to that elusive God along the way. His quest for an answer to the perennial problem of innocent suffering is as pressing in our day as ever it was in his. The current theology of his day, represented by his theologian 'friends,' Eliphaz, Bildad, Zophar, was that all suffering is the result of sin. There is no innocent suffering. Besides, it was believed, there is exact retribution: virtue is rewarded, wickedness punished – in this life. For, at the age of the Book of Job, there was no concept of life after death. (Our perception of an afterlife and of retribution beyond death should not dispose us to seek a facile solution to the problem). Job looked, dispassionately, at life, and declared with candour:

> It is all one; therefore I say, he destroys both the blameless and the wicked. When disaster brings sudden death, he mocks at the calamity of the innocent (9:22-23).

What an honest reaction to the unfairness of life. If, for us, with our belief in an afterlife, injustice in our world is still so painful, what must it have been for those, like the author of Job, for whom there was no afterlife?

Job turns out to be a believer who could sustain faith in a caring God when all experience pointed in another direction. His perplexity is highlighted in the outrageous passage where Job asked: 'Why are not times of judgment kept by the Almighty?' (24:1). Why is God not just! Job had, hitherto, subscribed to a theology that maintained that all suffering is due to sin. Here (24:1-12) he describes the arrogant aggression of the oppressor and the helpless suffering of the oppressed. And at the end he hurls his challenge at God:

> From out of the city the dying groan,
> and the soul of the wounded cries for help;
> yet God pays no attention to their prayer! (24:12).

The sheer honesty is heart-rending. How utterly different from another view:

> I was young and now I am old,
> but I have never seen the just man forsaken,
> nor his children begging for bread (Ps 37:25).

This is pathetic! It is a desperate clinging to a doctrinaire position in face of the evidence. But if your theology is neatly systematic – and your God predictible – you will, perforce, sacrifice fact to theory.

Before disaster struck, Job had shared the theology of his friends. Now, his experience has shown that theology to be flawed. We, (the readers) know that Job's sustained plea of innocence was authentic (Job 1-2). Neither Job nor his theologian friends were let in on the secret. Job experienced that the theology did not work. From their theological ivory tower the theologians confidently diagnosed Job's problem: he suffers *because* he is a sinner. The Book of Job is, and ever will be, a radical challenge to any theology that seeks to operate outside of experience.

More agonizing still for Job than his attempts to cope with the problems of retribution and innocent suffering was his sense of the absence of God. Job keeps crying out to a God who will not answer. His experience is a classic example of the 'dark night of the soul' described by later mystics. God had not withdrawn – but Job felt that he had. In reality he was, in his groping, growing closer all the time to that hidden God. His situation shouted that God is uncaring – callous even. Job's sturdy faith will not accept it to be so:

> If I go forward, he is not there;
> or backward, I cannot perceive him;
> on the left he hides and I cannot behold him;
> I turn to the right but I cannot see him.
> But he knows the way that I take;
> when he has tested me I shall come out like gold (23:8-10).

In his frustration and anger, Job yet came to glimpse the God veiled from the eyes of his theologically complacent friends. With wonder he recognized that God can be wholly preoccupied with one suffering human. He learned that the seemingly aloof and silent God was a God who willed to be within the human world. He chose to be present in the finitude and frailty of a powerless and afflicted human being. He is the God who is present to and in human suffering.

The climax of Job's joust with God comes in chapters 29-31. There he details his past happiness (29) – an ideal patriarchal lifestyle: rich in family, goods and esteem, his present misery (30), and swears a solemn oath of innocence (31). Chapter 30 is his lament. He suffers public contumely: where he had been formerly revered by the great, he is now despised and mocked by the meanest (30:1-15). Worst of all, by far, is the hostile presence of that absent God (vv. 16-22). He prays to God (vv. 20-23) – but does God listen?

> I cry to you alone and you do not answer me;
> I stand, and you merely look at me.
> You have turned cruel to me;
> with the might of your hand you persecute me (vv. 20-21).

God seems to have wholly ignored Job's compassion and concern for the poor (see 29:12-17):

> Did I not weep for those whose day was hard?
> Was not my soul grieved for the poor?
> But when I looked for good evil came;
> and when I waited for life, darkness came (vv. 24-25).

What kind of retribution is this! Job vehemently complains. The complaint is his prayer, giving tongue to his suffering. At last, the silent God speaks – and overwhelms Job! (chapters 38-41).

What is God's verdict on Job? It is unambiguous. In contrast the three staunch champions of theological orthodoxy fare very badly indeed. They had urged the cause of their God, a theoretical God. Job had rebelled: he sought the true God. To their shock Yahweh approves the outrageous Job and condemns their righteousness. Surely an anticipation of Jesus' view of things.

> The Lord said to Eliphaz: 'My wrath is kindled against you and your two friends; for you have not spoken of me what is right, as my servant Job has' (42:7).

Lamentations

Though traditionally attached to the book of Jeremiah (not, however, in the Hebrew Bible) *Lamentations* is not the work of the prophet. These five poems are laments for a fallen Jerusalem and destroyed temple composed by some who had been left in Jerusalem after the disaster of 587 B.C. They are communal laments arising out of the experience of distress. Survivors of the catastrophe – Nebuchadnezzar's conquest – speak their anguish: 'Jerusalem remembers, in the days of her affliction and wanderings ... ' (Lam 1:7). Through the laments, in the midst of pain, runs a sentiment of unshaken trust in God. They are in place in our liturgy of Holy Week.

Confession of sin does emerge in Lamentations: 'The Lord is in the right, for I have rebelled against his word' (1:18). More prominent, however, are complaints addressed directly to God as the one who has inflicted severe hardship on the people of God:

> The Lord has trodden as a wine press the virgin daughter of Judah (1:15).

> How the Lord in his anger has humiliated daughter Zion (2:1).

> The Lord has become like an enemy; he has destroyed Israel (2:5).

The complaint is balanced by yearning to return to the Lord:

> Cry aloud to the Lord! let tears stream down like a torrent

day and night! (2:18).

Let us test and examine our ways, and return to the Lord (3:40).

And, the confidence – the serene assurance:

> For the Lord will not reject forever;
> although he causes grief, he will have compassion
> according to the abundance of his steadfast love;
> for he does not willingly afflict or grieve anyone (3:31-33).

To the end, even in deep distress, the heartening note of complaint lingers:

> Why have you forgotten us completely? Why have you forsaken us these many days? Restore us to yourself, O Lord, that we may be restored! Renew our days as of old – unless you have utterly rejected us, and are angry with us beyond measure (5:20-22).

'Have you utterly rejected us?' It is not a rhetorical question. It carries overtones of exasperation worthy of Moses and Jeremiah. Here is a people bloody but unbowed – not in defiance of God but in robust confidence in his loving kindness.

> In the final analysis, those who have been smitten still hold fast in their lament – in their language of suffering – to the one who smote them ... Even though they have deserved their fate, they proceed to pour out their hearts to the very one who struck them down! It is this logic which leads them to cry, 'Woe to us' while at the same time pleading for mercy from the one against whom they have sinned! Here comes to the fore the other aspect of the divine action with regard to the people of God, namely the divine mercy upon those who beseech God in their suffering.[4]

4. C. Westermann, *Op. cit.*, 232.

Missing the point

Though confession of sin is, quite often, a constituent of lament, it is not always present. In not a few cases the lament carries a protestation of innocence. Job, for one, is emphatically consistent in his claim of innocence. Although so prevalent in the Old Testament, lament has not become part of Christian prayer. There is the fact, of course, that the Psalter is prominent in Christian worship. Psalms of lament figure largely. The truth is: they are not acknowledged as such. The Christian who, formally, prays a psalm of lament is, rarely, if ever, directing a passionate complaint to God – much less at God! It is precisely as uninhibited complaint that lament functions. We Christians simply miss the point.[5]

Perhaps it might be said that confession of sin has become the Christianized form of lament. Both in Christian theology and Christian worship suffering has receded into the background. It is stressed that Jesus Christ's work of salvation has to do with forgiveness of sin and eternal life. There is much less concern with the gospel witness to Jesus' total sensitivity towards human suffering. The result is that the 'sufferings of this world' are regarded as of little importance. Sin is what really matters. The believing Christian will not complain but will 'offer up' one's sufferings. It was something Jesus did not do! – Gethsemane and the cross! Indeed one may get the impression that though Jesus of Nazareth cared for those who suffered and pitied those who mourned, the risen Lord is preoccupied solely with sin. Claus Westermann has put it aptly:

5. 'A depreciatory attitude toward the lament reflects the fact that lamentation has been severed from prayer in Christian piety throughout the history of the church. In the Old Testament lamentation is an intrinsic component of prayer, as is shown in the Psalter, with its high percentage of psalms of lamentation. In the Christian church, on the other hand, the lament no longer receives a hearing. This transformation took place without being discussed in the official theologies of the church. Nowhere is there a reasoned rejection of lamentation as an intrinsic component of prayer; the severing of lamentation from prayer took place without comment.' C. Westermann, *Op. cit.*, 81-82.

There is no passage in the Gospels which suggests that Jesus saw his task to be one of convincing the sufferer that one must bear suffering patiently. There are narratives in which Jesus combines the forgiveness of sins with healing, but there are no narratives in which Jesus puts the forgiveness of sins in the place of healing.[6]

While the New Testament in no way prevents the Christian from lamenting, in practice, the lament has been excluded in Christian relationship with God, and has virtually disappeared from prayer and worship. This exclusion does not come from the New Testament. It is surely due to Greek influence: the Greek notion of God and the ethic of Stoicism. The Hebrew God is one who welcomes dialogue and invites plain speaking. Israel obliged! But, then, the God of Israel was a God who himself lamented.[7]

The fact is, we tend to be inhibited and formulistic in our prayer. We imagine that there is an appropriate manner of addressing God – a refined and courtly language befitting divinity. We expect God to conduct himself in a proper 'godly' manner and we assume that he wants us to be 'proper' in our approach to him. We learn from the Old Testament that Israel, with a more robust understanding of God, could dare to complain to God of God, could talk back at him without restraint. It is an approach endorsed by Jesus himself.

Jesus acknowledged that sufferers have the right to lament their suffering. He accepted lamentation as the language of suffering and thereby granted it both validity and dignity. The history of the people of God is grounded in the fact that God heard the lamentation of those who did not understand God but nonetheless cried out to God.

6. C.Westermann, *Praise and Lament in the Psalms*. (Edinburgh: T. & T. Clark, 1981), 275.
7. See W. Harrington, *The Tears of God*. (Collegeville: Liturgical Press, 1992), 26-37.

To such God came as Deliverer. It is with a cry out of the depths that each story of deliverance, each account of rescue, begins. The Bible speaks of God as One who is moved to compassion by the laments of those who suffer.[8]

Repentance

For the people of Israel, lament was a powerful way of prayer. It was a firm part of their tradition and, because of the prominence of lament in the Psalter, it was an abiding feature of their worship. There is, however, another, a different manner of talking to God. It is one thing to challenge him from the ground of striving to do his will. But when one is conscious of having failed, and failed dismally, what does one do? In this situation we find that post-exilic prayers (prayers in the aftermath of the sixth century Babylonian Exile) are encouragement and comfort. We have seen that Lamentations is a reaction to the Exile. In these other prayers the lament element is subdued or absent. They are straight-forward: we have sinned; we deserve all that has come upon us. Are we depressed? No! We acknowledge our sin, our shameful ingratitude – and we turn to God. We have sinned, we have failed – but you are *you*. It is, in some sort, an anticipation of: 'I shall arise and go to my Father.'

TRAUMA OF EXILE

The Lord said to Abraham: 'I will make nations of you, and kings shall come from you. I will establish my covenant between me and you, and your offspring after you throughout their generations, for an everlasting covenant, to be God to you and to your offspring after you' (Gen 17:6-7).

The Lord said to David: 'I will raise up your son after you ... and I will establish his kingdom ... your house and

8.   C. Westermann, *Lamentations*, 235.

your kingdom shall be made sure for ever before me; your throne shall be established for ever.' (2 Sam 7:12,16).

What was an Israelite to think when God's solemn promise to David had come to nothing? There was no questioning the harsh reality of Nebuchadnezzar's conquest: temple, city and nation were gone. On the strength of Yahweh's word it ought not to have been so; but it had happened. For the thoughtful Yahwist the disaster was a mirror held up to the nation, a mirror that showed a visage of gross failure and sin. Some, at least, had learned from the bitter experience of the Babylonian Exile: the faith answer to the disaster was repentance and hope. The people had failed – of that there could be no doubt. But Yahweh was steadfast as ever. There was a way of restoration, a way of redemption. It was the way of candid confession of sin and of total trust in God's boundless mercy. The many moving post-exilic prayers to be found in Baruch, Ezra and Nehemiah, Tobit and Sirach, Esther and Judith and the Book of Daniel firmly follow this way.[9]

While post-exilic prayers tend to be lengthy, there is about them a refreshing candour and an inspiring faith. They are the prayers of a chastened people, a people that, in adversity, had found its soul. Those who pray confess sin openly. They do not grovel, but maintain a quiet dignity. Most instructive is a recurring phrase that characterizes God as 'the great and awesome God who keeps covenant and steadfast love with those who love him and keep his commandments' – followed always by the confession: 'We have sinned.' These later Israelites had come to understand that the 'awesome God' is such only to those who have never known him. Those who pray these prayers have discovered the way of restoration, the way of redemption.

Another appendix to Jeremiah (besides Lamentations) is Baruch – a writing much later than the age of Jeremiah's

9. Baruch 1:15-3-8; Ezra 9:6-15; Neh 1:5-11; 9:6-37; Tobit 13:1-8; Sirach 36:1-17; Esther 13:9-17; 14:3-19; Judith 9:2-14; Daniel 3:26-45; 9:4-19.

disciple-secretary. Its author is very conscious of the contrast between the holy God and his sinful people: 'The Lord our God is in the right, but there is open shame on us and our ancestors this very day' (Bar 2:6; see 1:15).

The introduction to this prayer (1:15 - 2:10) is a candid confession of sin: 'We have not entreated the favour of the Lord by turning away, each of us, from the thoughts of our wicked hearts ... We have not obeyed his voice, to walk in the statutes of the Lord which he set before us' (Bar 2:8,10). The prayer itself (2:11 - 3:8) recalls the great Exodus event. That is the basis of the exiled people's confidence, not necessarily that they be restored to their homeland, but that in exile they may meet their God.

> O Lord Almighty, God of Israel, the soul in anguish and the wearied spirit cry out to you. Hear, O Lord, and have mercy, for we have sinned before you ... Do not remember the iniquities of our ancestors, but in this crisis remember your power and your name. For you are the Lord our God, and it is you, O Lord, whom we will praise. For you have put the fear of you in our hearts so that we would call upon your name; and we will praise you in our exile, for we have put away from our hearts all the iniquity of our ancestors who sinned against you (3:1-2, 5-7).

DANIEL

The purpose of the Book of Daniel was to bolster the faith that was in danger of being stamped out by the aggression of Antiochus Epiphanes (175-163 B.C.), the Seleucid ruler. The author wanted to hearten his people and urge them to unyielding loyalty. He wholeheartedly supported the Maccabean revolt (167-164 B.C.). He based his summons to courageous faith on the conviction that God ruled the course of history. Yet, the prayers in the book acknowledge without excuse the failures of Israel and appeal solely to the graciousness of Yahweh. Such is the prayer of Azariah (Dan 3:26-45):

'For you are just in all you have done ... for we have sinned and broken your law in turning away from you; in all matters we have sinned grievously (3:27-29). Confession of sin is but a prelude to confident hope:

> Yet with a contrite heart and a humble spirit may we be accepted, as though it were with burnt offerings of rams and bulls, or with tens of thousands of fat lambs; such may our sacrifice be in your sight today, and may we unreservedly follow you, for no shame will come to those who trust in you. And now with all our heart we follow you; we fear you and seek your presence. Do not put us to shame, but deal with us in your patience and in your abundant mercy (3:39- 42).

The epitome of these post-exilic prayers is Daniel 9:4-19. This prayer is not only typical, it is the most moving of all these prayers of the chastened. But we would instance another prayer – the apocryphal Prayer of Manasseh. In 2 Kings 21, Manasseh (687-642 B.C.) is presented as the most wicked of the kings of Judah. This is repeated in 2 Chronicles 33. The Chronicler, however, tells of Manasseh's conversion and makes reference to his prayer of repentance (2 Chron 33:10-19). A later writer supplied an appropriate prayer, a worthy example of post-exilic piety, a prayer of repentance more moving than the *Miserere* (Psalm 51). Some excerpts will make the point.

> Immeasurable and unsearchable is your promised mercy, for you are the Lord Most High, of great compassion, long- suffering, and very merciful ... You, O Lord, according to your great goodness have promised repentance and forgiveness to those who have sinned against you; and in the multitude of your mercies you have appointed repentance for sinners, that they may be saved ... you have appointed repentance for me, who am a sinner ... And now I bend the knee of my heart, beseeching you for your

kindness. I have sinned, O Lord I have sinned, and I know my transgressions. I earnestly beseech you, forgive me, O Lord, forgive me! For you, O Lord, are the God of those who repent, and in me you will manifest your goodness; for unworthy as I am, you will save me in your great mercy, and I will praise you continually all the days of my life.

If even Manasseh (who gets such a bad press in Kings and Chronicles), after turning back to the Lord, could feel so confident of salvation, there is hope for any and every sinner!

The God who grieves

Lament and Repentance: there is no conflict. I can know that I am a sinner. It may well be that my sufferings are due to my frailty. I must be sure that they are not sanctions imposed by a judgmental God. This, of course, runs counter to the current view in Israel, illustrated in these prayers, that personal and national disaster was divine punishment.

There has ever been the human tendency to picture God as offended, angered even, by human sin. The truth is: sin, whatever form it takes, is an affront to God's plan for his creation. And God, the Creator, *grieves* over sin. There is grief and sadness, and suffering, in the heart of God. There is no wrath, no anger. With infinite patience he bears with us, not infringing on the freedom with which he has endowed us, but respecting our dignity. He is grieved at the sheer burden of sin that weighs upon us. He is constantly calling out to us: 'Here am I, here am I' (Isa 65:1). He waits for our response, waits not only in patience but with divine compassion. I come before my God as sinner. I come, humbly, but with a dignity that becomes him and me. And, sinner though I am, I can cry out at the unfairness of suffering.

We are children of God: *sinful children*. We have not responded fittingly to his goodness; we have taken advantage of his love. We are sorry, or ought to be, for our failures.

But our God does not want us to feel guilt. He is a God of compassion who is with us in our sorrow. He is a God of forgiveness, and his forgiveness is prompt and total. We, then, should have the decency – the humility – to acknowledge our failures: 'God, be merciful to me, a sinner.'

Merciful to All

> For God has imprisoned all in disobedience,
> that he may be merciful to all
> (Romans 11:32).

Our study thus far has established that God is fully deter-mined to have the last word. This is, of course, is as it should be. More importantly, it is truly Good News. What we have perceived of the sheer graciousness of God would urge us to see it so. Israel, notably in prayer of lament, had discerned this. There is robust faith and firm hope in the plaintive 'Why' and 'How long.' There is a holy impatience to it. It springs from the conviction that God can do better, much better, than he is doing. There is nothing mean-spirited in the repentance of Israel. Confession of sin carries the assurance that sin has been forgiven. The prophets have consistently perceived word of divine mercy beyond warning and threat – beyond even divine chastisement as they reckoned it. The question, then, arises: will God's word of mercy eventually embrace all of humankind?

A vital factor here is human freedom and God's utter respect of our freedom. Precisely because of the freedom factor, it is not possible to say, definitely, that salvation will be universal. But, when one focuses on God, then one may appropriately hope for the salvation of the whole human race. It is not a vain hope. It carries impressive scriptural warranty.

Universal Salvation
If salvation means fellowship with God and blessedness of eternal life with God, universal salvation means that all

human beings will eventually be redeemed by God's gracious love – a love displayed ultimately in Jesus Christ. On the other hand, a limited salvation view assumes that only those who, in this life, acknowledge the true God, and in the Christian Scripture setting, confess Christ as Lord – will finally be saved. Both views – limited salvation and universal salvation – are found prominently in both Old Testament and New Testament. A stream of texts maintains that final salvation is limited (e.g. Isa 26: 20-21; 66:15-16; Matt 25: 31-46; John 3:36). Another stream suggests or affirms universal salvation (e.g. Isa 66: 18-23; John 3:17; Rom 11:32-36; 1 Tim 2:3-4). In some cases, both views are juxtaposed. For example, Isaiah says:

> For the Lord will come in fire …
> to pay back his anger in fury …
> For by fire will the Lord execute judgment,
> and by his sword, on all flesh;
> and those slain by the sword shall be many (Isa 66:15-16).

Immediately afterward, Isaiah 66:18-23, we read:

> I am coming to gather all nations and tongues;
> and they shall come and shall see my glory, and I will set a sign among them. From them I will send survivors to the nations … to the coastlands far away that have not heard of my fame or seen my glory; and they shall declare my glory among the nations.

Or, again, John 3:36:

> Whoever believes in the Son has eternal life; whoever disobeys the Son will not see life, but must endure God's wrath.

This stands in sharp contrast to the statement a few verses earlier (3:17):

> Indeed, God did not send the Son into the world to

condemn the world, but in order that the world might be saved through him.

For the rest, it will suffice to quote some of the texts that , arguably, point towards universal salvation, before going on to take a closer look at the more notable of them.

Ps 86:9   All the nations you have made shall come
               and bow down before you, O Lord,
               and shall glorify your name.

Isa 25:6,8.   On this mountain the Lord of hosts will make
               for all peoples a feast of rich food ...

               And the Lord will wipe away the tears from
               all faces.

Isa 52:10.   The Lord has bared his holy arm before the
               eyes of all the nations;

               and all the ends of the earth shall see the
               salvation of our God.

Isa 66:18,23.   I am coming to gather all nations and tongues;
               and they shall come and shall see my glory ...

               From new moon to new moon, and from
               sabbath to sabbath, all flesh shall come to
               worship before me, says the Lord.

Jn 12:32.   And I, when I am lifted up from the earth, will
               draw all people to myself.

1 Cor 15:22,28 For as all die in Adam, so will all be made alive
               in Christ ... When all things are subjected to
               him, then the Son himself will also be sub-
               jected to the one who puts all things in subjec-
               tion under him, so that God may be all in all.

Phil 2:10-11   ... so that at the name of Jesus every knee
               should bend, in heaven and on earth and

under the earth, and every tongue confess that Jesus Christ is Lord, to the glory of God the Father.

1 Tim 2:3-4   This is right and acceptable in the sight of God our Saviour, who desires all to be saved.

1 Tim 4:10   ... we have our hope set on the living God, who is the Saviour of all people, especially of those who believe.

Tit 2:11.   For the grace of God has appeared, bringing salvation to all.

Paul

Arguably, the weightiest text of all in favour of universal salvation is found in Paul. One may well consider that Romans 9-11 is not the easiest section of Paul's writings. But one cannot fail to be stirred by the passion behind these pages. Paul simply will not accept that God has rejected his people (Rom 11:1).

His argument throughout is tortuous because the problem he addresses is so puzzling: How could God's people have failed to recognize God's final Messenger? He wrestles over an Israel gone astray: 'I have great sorrow and unceasing anguish in my heart ... [on behalf of] my own people, my kindred according to the flesh' (9:2-3). Although 'from them, according to the flesh, comes the Messiah' (9:5) they will not acknowledge Jesus as that Messiah. Throughout chapters 9-11 he proposes one 'logical' argument after another to account for their obduracy. Happily, his 'logic' was flawed from the start because he stolidly refused to entertain the 'obvious' conclusion that they had been rejected for their unfaith. 'I ask, then, has God rejected his people? By no means! ... God has not rejected his people whom he foreknew' (11:1-2). At the end, he threw logic out the window and spoke with prophetic conviction: 'And so all Israel will be saved' (11:26). He had taken his stand on an impregnable theological base: 'for the gifts and calling of God are irrevocable' (11:29). The incorrigibly illogical God is the utterly constant God.

In Romans 11:25 Paul states:

> I want you to understand this mystery; a hardening has come upon part of Israel, until the full number of the Gentiles has come in.

'Mystery' is revelation of God's plan of grace. The content of that 'mystery' is the hardening of Israel! Here, indeed, is a paradox of mercy. Paul Achtemeier has put it finely:

> From the stuff of human disobedience, God has shaped the means of his mercy (v. 32). That is the conclusion to which Paul comes in this passage [11:25-36] ... Mercy is God's response to disobedient Israel as it is his response to disobedient gentiles ... If it seems a strange way to go about the redemption of creation ... it is a striking example of the omnipotence of God.[1]

Throughout chapters 9-11 Paul wrestled with a humanly incomprehensible situation, but never loosened his grip on his conviction of God's utter faithfulness. At the end, he committed the whole matter to God and declared, in words that had little to do with the forced logic of his argument up to now: 'and so all Israel will be saved' (11:26). A remarkable statement. Then, Paul took a truly giant step: 'For God has imprisoned all in disobedience so that he may be merciful to all' (11:32). His declaration has to be seen in contrast to the unrelieved picture he had painted in Romans 1-3 – all humankind stands under Sin (*Hamartia* -- Sin – is regarded as a tyrannical power), cut off from God. But, then, that backdrop was designed to highlight the incredible graciousness of God (to be presented in chapters 5 to 8). It is not surprising

---

1. *Romans* (Atlanta: John Knox Press, 1985), p. 187.

that Paul closes with an awe-inspired doxology:

> O the depth of the riches and wisdom and knowledge of
> God! How unsearchable are his judgments and how in-
> scrutable his ways!
>> For who has known the mind of the Lord?
>> Or who has been his counsellor?
>> Or who has given a gift to him, to receive a gift in
>> return?
> For, for him and through him and to him are all things.
> To him be glory forever. Amen. (11:33-36).

The inscrutable way of God is his unfailing word of salvation.[2]

Revelation

Some have found in the Book of Revelation a doctrine of
universal salvation. At first blush, suggestion of such a
presence must seem absurd. Revelation appears to display
such a spirit of vindictiveness and, seemingly, revels so in
the destruction of earth and its inhabitants that it can scarcely
be taken for a Christian book. Closer study, based on an
appreciation of its apocalyptic genre and of the purpose of
the writing, as well as of a strong prophetic element, does
lead to a different assessment.[3] Revelation is a thoroughly

2. 'Because God can use even rebellion and disobedience in his plan of
   mercy on all, we may have utter confidence in that God, however his
   plan may seem to be going awry. Nothing, not even the rejection of his
   own Son by his own people could affect God's purposes of grace. If God's
   ways are past finding out, his mercy is past any impeding. God is faithful
   to his purposes of mercy, and he is capable of carrying out his plan,
   whatever the reaction of his creation may be to those purposes. Trust in
   such a God is an eminently reasonable act, since he is reliable and
   unwavering in his purpose of mercy for his creation and is totally
   capable of bringing that mercy to reality. It is that assurance that Paul
   sings forth in the closing hymn of verses 33-36. God is the source,
   sustainer, and goal of all things. What a glorious God!' P. Achtemeir, *Op.
   cit.*, p. 189.
3. See W.J.Harrington, *Revelation*. Sacra Pagina 16 (Collegeville: Liturgical
   Press, 1993; W. Harrington, *Revelation. Proclaiming a Vision of Hope* (San
   Jose: Resource Publications, 1994).

Christian writing which, despite first impression, carries a message of startling hope.

We find in Revelation, as elsewhere, texts which imply or assert limited salvation (e.g. 14:9-10; 20:11-15) and texts which imply or assert universal salvation (e.g. 1:7; 5:13; 14:6-7; 21:24-27). While this juxtaposition of seemingly contradictory views is not unique to John (as we have observed) he offers a key to his procedure in his judgment scene of 20:11-15, where he contrasts 'books' and the 'book of life.' People were judged by what they had done ('according to their works as written in the books'); yet, what is ultimately decisive is whether one's name is inscribed in the book of life. John maintains this tension throughout. In consciously paradoxical language and imagery he seeks, on the one hand to present human responsibility, and on the other hand to portray the finally victorious mercy of a gracious God.

For our purpose, the relevant factor is that a stream, sometimes hidden, yet flowing in steadfast hope, wends through the sombre landscape of Revelation. Could it be otherwise for one who had discerned the conquering God in the Lamb who was slain?

> John knows that for Christians the question of universal or limited salvation is not an abstract speculative question, addressing the question of 'How many?' It is rather faith's confession of the meaning of the act of God in Christ; the God whose victory does not depend on ours, who loves us when we do not love him or ourselves, who believes in us when we do not believe in him or ourselves, who saves us when we do not believe we need saving or are worth saving.[4]

TEXTS CONCERNING SALVATION

1:7   Behold, he will come with the clouds, and every eye will see him, even those who pierced him, and all the

4.   M. E. Boring, *Revelation* (Louisville: John Knox, 1989).

tribes of the earth will wail because of him. So be it. Amen.

The text is based on a combination of Daniel 7:3 and Zechariah 12:10, a combination which occurs also in Matthew 24:30. When the Christ makes his appearance he will be manifest to all, even to them whose hostility numbers them with those who had encompassed his death; 'all the tribes of the earth' (see 5:9; 7:9; 14:6) does not have the pejorative sense of 'the inhabitants of the earth' (enemies of God and Lamb). The 'tribes' are, simply, the whole of humankind. 'Wail because of him'; does this 'wailing' mean despairing lamentation in view of impending condemnation of their former rejection of the Lamb, or contrite lamentation for what they had done to him? In Zechariah 12:10 the context is penitential grief, and this is the better sense here: the tribes of the earth will lament in remorse.

5:13 Then I heard all creatures, in heaven and on earth and under the earth and in the sea crying: Blessing and honour, glory and might, to the One seated on the throne and to the Lamb for ever and ever!

Chapters four and five of Revelation, closely related, each end on a universal note (4:11; 5:13). 'I heard all creatures': the whole of creation, without exception, joins in the great canticle of praise. John hears the chorus of acclamation; to it the 'four living creatrues,' heavenly representatives of the created universe, give their 'Amen' – and the elders (the heavenly counterpart of the Church) worship. It is universal response: no one and nothing is excluded. The implication is that no part of creation is ultimately rebellious and lost.[5]

---

5. '[S]uch is John's confidence in the universality of Christ's achievement that his vision cannot stop short of universal response.' (G. B. Caird, *The Revelation of Saint John the Divine*, London: A. & C. Black, 1966, p. 77) 'Absolutely no one and nothing is excluded from this picture. Given this mind-expanding picture, it is impossible to see any part of the universe as ultimately rebellious and lost.' (M. E. Boring, *Op. cit.*, p. 112).

14:6-7 Then I saw another angel flying in mid-heaven, with an eternal gospel to proclaim to the inhabitants of the earth, to every nation, tribe, tongue and people. He cried with a loud voice, 'Fear God and give him glory; for the hour of his judgment has come. Worship him who made heaven and earth, the sea and the springs of water'.

The angel flies in mid-heaven – the zenith – because his proclamation is of universal import. 'Gospel (*euangelion*) can only mean 'good news.' The invitation is addressed to all of humankind, including 'the inhabitants of the earth' – a phrase which, throughout Revelation, designates those who follow the Beast (3:10; 11:10; 13:8, 12, 14; 17:2, 8). They are urged to 'fear God and give him glory' (see 11:13) – they are being called to repentance, to *metanoia* (see Mark 1:14-15). The offer of repentance and salvation precedes the judgment; the proclamation of the 'gospel' heralds the time of salvation.[6]

15:3b-4 Just and true are your ways, O king of the nations. Who shall not fear you, Lord, and do homage to your name? For you alone are holy. All nations will come and worship before you, for your righteous deeds have been revealed.

While most manuscripts read 'king of the ages,' the better reading is, surely, 'king of the nations.' The song holds out hope that the nations, in view of the judgments of the Lord, will fear (that is, reverence) him and render him homage and worship. In other words, God is King of the nations, and the nations will come to acknowledge him as their King. Our God, even in judgment, is always in the business of salvation

---

6. 'The first angel is depicted as proclaiming the "gospel," the eternal good news, to all the people on earth. The gospel given by the angel is that the time of salvation is at hand ... The angel is summoning the whole world to pay homage to its victorious creator.' (P. Perkins, *The Book of Revelation* Collegeville MN: Liturgical Press, 1983, p. 64).

– a God bent on the salvation of humankind.[7]

21:3   I heard a loud voice from the throne say:
       Behold, God's dwelling is with humankind!
       He will dwell among them and they will be his
           peoples,
       and God himself will be with them as their God.

Again we have a variant reading, 'his peoples' – the plural instead of the singular 'people.' John's source is Ezekiel 37:27: 'My dwelling place shall be with them; and I will be their God, and they shall be my people.' John has extended the prophet's promise to Israel ('people') to all humankind. John utters the promise that God will dwell among his peoples. He was never God of Israel only; he is not prepared to be God of Christians only.

21:24-27 The nations will walk by its light and the kings of
          the earth will bring their glory into it. Its gates will
          never be shut by day – for there will be no night
          there. They will bring into it the splendour and
          wealth of the nations, but nothing unclean will
          enter it, nor any who practise abomination or
          falsehood, but only those who are written in the
          Lamb's book of life.

John is manifestly inspired by Isaiah 60. Unlike Isaiah, he is here describing the heavenly Jerusalem. Its inhabitants are not drawn from all nations – they are the nations and the kings of the earth – thus fulfilling the universalist prophecies of Jewish Scripture. The divine light of the city ('the glory of God gave it light, and its lamp was the Lamb, v. 23) is a beacon to the nations. These are the same 'nations' and

---

7. 'We must accept this optimism as an essential part of John's theology.
    There are a few passages like this in his book where he speaks unequivo-
    cally and without the cloak of symbol, and, instead of ignoring them or
    treating them as erratic and inconsequent intrusions, we ought to allow
    them to control our interpretation of his symbolism.' (G. B. Caird, *Op. cit.*,
    p. 199)

'kings' that had opposed God's rule and made war on the Lamb and his followers (15:14; 17:18; 18:9; 19:19; 20:8) – the very nations and kings destroyed in the great eschatological battle! (19:21; 20:9) The reference to 'nothing unclean' within the city is to be read as a pastoral warning to John's readers. The kingdom of God is not for such as those listed; Christians must seek, here and now, to break with sin.

Matthew 25

This has been a selection, no more, but enough to have made a point. And the point is that, when one looks more closely at Revelation, beyond the imagery of violence one finds, firmly expressed, a prospect of universal salvation. Since the alternative would seem to be, for some at least, eternal damnation, it is helpful, for the sake of perspective, to examine a celebrated Matthaean passage.

Straightway: a problem. Can one, as a Christian, really believe that the suffering Jesus on the cross who in Luke's passion-story prayed: 'Father, forgive them; for they do not know what they do' (Lk 23:34) could, as risen Lord, declare in awful judgment: 'Depart from me you cursed, into the eternal fire'? Matthew, it seems (25:41) would have us think so. That such is really his intent becomes incredible when we understand that the 'they' of Luke's text embraces all who brought Jesus to death. Jesus prays forgiveness for the obdurate chief priests and their allies. Luke is suggesting that even perpetrators of evil never really appreciate God's goodness or the strange wisdom of his purpose. Besides, we should view this seemingly irrevocable sentence (Mt 25:41) against what we know of the Old Testament and of the New. God is the God whose heart 'recoils' at the prospect of losing Ephraim (Hos 11:8); the God who desires the salvation of all (1 Tim 2:4); the God who did not spare his own Son (John 3:16). Surely Jesus would have us believe that his God and ours loves us with divine love beyond our imagining.

Still, what are we to make of Matthew's Last Judgment

(25:31-46)? We are to understand it as myth. Myth is a symbolic form of expression couched in narrative which is not intended to be historical. It deals with realities which transcend experience – in this case the reality of definitive encounter with God.

In effect, the 'last judgment' is warning: it primarily relates to one's conduct in the present. One is challenged to live in such a way that, should it occur, one would not be caught unawares. While the King stresses his solidarity with 'all,' the exhortation is, by Matthew, addressed to Christians. We are being taught how we should prepare for the 'coming' of the Lord, prepared for our meeting with him. The 'last judgment' is taking place in my life here and now. The 'books' are being written. But, has my name 'been written in the book of life since the foundation of the world' (Rev 17:8)? There is the true judgment.

Hell

Last Judgment conjures up visions of heaven and hell. The terms 'heaven' and 'hell' are, obviously, human words – and the accompanying imaginings are all too human.

Humans, not God, have invented hell. Theologically, what the terms signify is the reality of human decisions for good and evil and consequent human possibilities. Contemporary theology, on the basis of human freedom, and of God's total respect for freedom, regards hell as a possibility.[8]

8. 'The message of hell has to do with the seriousness with which we view human life and with the possibility of total failure in working out the project of human life … The possibility of hell cannot be denied without denying human freedom itself. But if freedom itself is incalculable, then it is impossible to say definitely whether salvation will be universal. Christians can appropriately hope for the salvation of the entire human race. They cannot know definitely whether, in fact, that will be the outcome of history. The traditional language of hell and punishment holds before us the negative possibility of human freedom. Thus, contemporary theology is inclined to interpret the teaching of the church as referring to the possibility of hell.' (Z. Hayes, 'Hell' in J. Komonchak, M. Collins, D. Lane, eds,, *The New Dictionary of Theology*, Wilmington, DE: M. Glazier, 1987, p. 459)

God alone knows if a human being can definitively choose evil – and only in such a case is there the possibility of 'hell'. Still, the prospect of heaven and hell is salutary, pointing up the seriousness of decision in the present.[9]

In a theological reflection on hell, Edward Schillebeeckx quotes a saying of Therese of Lisieux, 'Je crois dans l'enfer, mais je crois qu'il est vide' – 'I believe in hell, but I believe there's no one in it' – and characterizes it as anything but unbiblical. He also adverts to the *apokatastasis* of some Church Fathers – in the end everyone will be saved – and to the similar implication of the doctrine of reincarnation in non-Christian religions. His unease is that such solutions suggest too cheap an estimation of mercy and forgiveness.[10] He proposes his own view with characteristic theological perspicacity and verve. I believe that he offers a satisfying theological answer to the question raised by the optimistic stream in Revelation (and elsewhere). And, in so doing, he raises, by implication, the further question whether 'universal salvation' is an appropriate label for what we have been considering under that rubric.

Heaven and hell are symbols, but they are not on the same level – they are asymmetrical affirmations of faith. The basis of 'eternal life' – that is what 'heaven' means – is living communion with God. God is source of that bond of life which is already a reality during earthly life, a bond which cannot be snapped at death. Living communion with the

9. I have offered a rather loose paraphrase of a more theologically precise text: 'Goodness and evil, "heaven" and "hell", are in the first place anthropological possibilities, in other words, decisions by men and women themselves. Not God, but human beings, are the inventors of hell, precisely by the way they behave. In their situated freedom, human beings are in fact in a position to do both good and evil. Whether there are in fact people who definitively choose evil I do not know; a judgment on that belongs only to God. But on the basis of human possibilities the biblical threats and perspectives of "heaven and hell" are a therapeutic and pedagogically meaningful perspective on the future. They really point towards something.' (E. Schillebeeckx, *Church: The Human Story of God*, London: SCM Press, 1990, p. 136).

10. *Op. cit.*, pp. 134-139.

living God abides beyond death. So there is heaven. There can be no hell on the same level. For, if living communion with God is the foundation of eternal life, the absence of such communion is the basis of non-eternal life. There is no longer any ground of eternal life. 'That seems to me to be the "second death" of the fundamental, definitive sinner (if there is such a person). That is "hell": not sharing in eternal life; not being someone who is tortured eternally – but no longer existing at death. That is the biblical "second death" (Rev 20:6).'[11] The evil have excluded themselves from communion with the living God – excluded themselves from life. They no longer exist. To choose hell is to choose a totally isolated existence. To reject God is to reject Being itself; it is to opt for nothingnesas. Hell is the condition of nonbeing; it is not a place or state. 'There is no shadow kingdom of hell next to the eternally happy kingdom of God. That is inherent in the asymmetry between what we call heaven and hell.'[12]

A mistake of the past has been to set good and evil on the same level. Evil, as distinct from good, is not something positive; it is the absence of good.[13] Here is the solid Thomistic basis of Schillebeeckx' position. There is nothing in evil that can mark it out for eternal life. Through its inherent emptiness the wicked world disappears by its own logic into absolutely nothing. Schillebeeckx claims, and I concur, that, in contrast to the model of the past – the traditional 'hell' – he offers a more plausible Christian solution to the problem of evil. And he concludes:

> So there is no future for evil and oppression, while goodness still knows a future beyond the boundary of death, thanks to the outstretched hand of God which receives us. God does not take vengeance; he leaves evil to its own, limited logic! So there is in fact an eternal difference

11. E. Schillebeeckx, *Op. cit.*, p. 137.
12. E. Schillebeeckx, *Op. cit.*, p. 137f.
13. Thomas Aquinas, *Summa Theologiae*, Ia. q.48, art. 5.

between good and evil, between the pious and the wicked (the deepest intent of the distinction between heaven and hell), but the pious continue to be spared having to rejoice over the torture of eternal doom being inflicted on their fellow human beings. God's unassailable holiness consists, rather, in the fact that he will not compel anyone to enter the kingdom of heaven as the unique kingdom of liberated and free people. The 'eschaton' or the ultimate is exclusively positive. There is no negative eschaton. Good, not evil, has the last word. That is the message and the distinctive human praxis of Jesus of Nazareth, whom Christians therefore confess as the Christ.[14]

There is no negative *eschaton*. This, it seems to me, is a better way of describing what we have been studying under the rubric 'universal salvation'. The trouble with the expression 'universal salvation' is that it might be taken in a manner that trivializes the deadly conflict between good and evil in our history and cheapens our view of God's mercy and forgiveness. God, not evil, has the last word. God's saving purpose for humankind – the *Eschaton*, the End – is salvation. There is no negative *eschaton*: God does not will damnation. For that matter, 'positive *eschaton* only' might be a better way of stating what 'universal salvation' is meant to express. Salvation is offered to all. But God is God of freedom; he will not compel. Whether any person, faced with Infinite Love, can choose to embrace evil – and, at some point, the choice must be stark: anything less would be unworthy of our God – we do not know. God and the Lamb alone know what names are inscribed in the book of life (see Rev 2o:11-15; 17:8). And, appreciating something of the foolishness of God,[15] one rather suspects that the names of all humans will be read there.

14. *Op. cit.,* 138f.
15. 'We proclaim Christ crucified … Christ the power of God and the wisdom of God. For God's foolishness is wiser than human wisdom, amd God's weakness is stronger than human strength' (1 Cor 1:23-25).

4

God's Foolishness

For God's foolishness is wiser than human wisdom,
and God's weakness is stronger than human strength
(1 Corinthians 1:25).

An investigation of the prophets, highlighting a remarkably consistent feature, points, inexorably, to a God whose last word is mercy and forgiveness. Indeed, we have seen that, arguably, God's plan for humankind, his goal of positive eschaton only, has issue in universal salvation. And there is the matter of response to God, by way of robust lament and dignified repentance. One may not, however, ignore other images of God and less worthy reactions to God. In this chapter one would seek, in some fashion, to pull these issues together. To do that is to glance at where the story ends for all of us – or begins! At the close there must be advertance to God's revelation of himself, in our history, in the man Jesus of Nazareth. Advertance only – anything further would merit another book ... or more.

God Is Love

God is love. That assertion can be a cliche – or it may be meaningful. Our normal experience of love is human love. Love can be limited and flawed – frequently possessive and stifling. Even at its finest it has the inevitable limitation of finitude. Divine love is wholly beyond our ken. It is not beyond our experience. I can be (indeed, ought to be) quite sure that God loves me. I cannot know divine love – because I cannot know God. Paul had understood: 'O the depth of the riches and wisdom and knowledge of God! How unsearchable are his judgments and how inscrutable his ways!' (Rom 11:33).

Our tendency is to limit the reach of God's love. Our traditional theology tells us that what we term 'mortal' sin cuts us off from God's love. It places a barrier between us and God. Regularly, this has been taken to mean that God has shut us off. This is gross misunderstanding. If there is barrier, it is of our devising. God does not build barriers. The gospels firmly depict Jesus – 'the reflection of God's glory and the exact imprint of God's very being' (Hebrews 1:3) – as 'friend of sinners.' A friend is one who loves. Jesus' love of sinners was scandal to the righteous. It was scandal far more disturbing than they had suspected. Because what Jesus proclaimed, in word and praxis, was God's preferential option for sinners!

Paul, as usual, had caught the point. In Romans 1-3 he painted, in unrelieved gloomy colour, the human lot: a humankind in thrall to the tyranny of Hamartia – 'all, both Jews and Greeks, are under the power of Sin' (Rom 3:9). It is humankind wholly estranged from God. This estranged humankind is, emphatically, not beyond the range of God's love:

> While we were still weak, at the right time Christ died for the ungodly (i.e. the estranged from God) … God proves his love for us in that while we were still sinners Christ died for us' (5:6,8).

Could anything be clearer? See Romans 8:31-39.

Creator
God is Creator and Saviour. He brought creation into being, creation with its own character and its potential for development. As Creator he has infinite respect for his creation; he loves his creation and wholly honours its freedom. Modern science has given us wonderful insights into God's world. Astronomy has alerted us to the fantastic size of the universe

and the seemingly limitless number of suns and planets. At the other end, science has opened up for us the remarkable intricacy of atoms and molecules.

In all this our God is not an absentee landlord; he is immediately present with his creation, in its joy and in its suffering. Claus Westermann[1] has alerted us to the danger of a one-sided reading of Genesis 1-3 - the reading of the text with almost exclusively anthropological focus. We must take seriously the refrain, 'God saw that it was good,' leading to the climax; 'God saw everything that he had made, and indeed, it was very good' (1:31). God has respect for the whole of his creation. And this respectful God is not intrusive. Yet, the Genesis stories, both in chapter 1 and chapter 2, make clear that, in the world we know, humankind is God's pride and joy. Humankind is also his supreme headache. God created with divine abandon, with divine magnanimity. He made humans free. He has scrupulously respected human freedom. He has paid a heavy price - the price of his unfailing love.

Deus Humanissimus

In traditional theology, God is a changeless God. This alleged immutability of God may make some sense in a context of Greek metaphysics. It does not fit in a context of biblical theology. The Yahweh of Israel, the Abba of Jesus, is not the Unmoved Mover of Aristotle but the God of Abraham and Moses.

The God of our faith is not a Greek God but a Hebrew God. Sadly, that Greek God has prevailed. The Greek God is Olympian, remote, remorselessly logical, impassible, totally humourless and touchy about his divinity. The Hebrew God is exuberantly illogical, immediate, can change his mind whenever he likes, suffers *because of, with* and *for* his people, has a refined sense of humour and has little interest in

---

1. *Genesis 1-11. A Commentary* (London: SPCK, 1984), pp. 173-177.

covering his divine back. There is a *God!* The God of biblical revelation is not a God who stands aloof from his creation. He is a passionate God, deeply in love with the work of his hands. And, throughout the Bible, is the refreshing anthropomorphism that keeps our God real and immediate.

Apopathic theology – the Latin *via negativa* (one can really only say what God is *not*) – is all very well. Indeed, it is salutary, reminding us that we never *know* God. But this is surely not at the price of blunting biblical imagery. The writers of the Old Testament – poets many of them – were wholly sure that their God was God. Though they would not have recognized the term, their God was, emphatically, a *transcendent* God. Their conviction is summed up in a title favoured by Second Isaiah: the Holy One of Israel – a transcendent God, preoccupied with his people. That is just the point. Our God is not a remote God. Our God is a God who *feels*, who *loves* and *suffers*. If this is so of Israel, what of the God who, through Jesus of Nazareth, has entered so wholly into our history? In Jesus, 'the reflection of God's glory and the exact imprint of God's very being' (Heb 1:3) we see the visage of our God. He is the *Deus humanissimus*. The inspired paradox of Schillebeeckx is a definition of God which matches that implied by the Abba title given to his God by Jesus of Nazareth.

The Graciousness of God

Nothing escapes the eye of God. How regularly this observation has been cast as sanction, as threat. Jesus' perspective was quite other. 'Your Father who sees in secret will reward you' (Mt 6: 4,6,18). 'Whoever gives even a cup of cold water to one of these little ones in the name of a disciple – truly I tell you, none of these will lose their reward' (10:42).

God does indeed keep a close eye on us – but to acknowledge whatever good we do. Our good works carry no price tag; there is no 'merit' in that sense. What is so much more important is 'recompense:' generous acknowledgment by a generous God. To his eye, nothing of good we do is unobserved or unimportant. Not surprisingly because, wherever there is good, it is of God. There are many, very many, who feel that they do not know God, yet, in fact, who witness to him – by doing good. They may not know God, but God knows them, and rejoices in them.

For one who claims to know God, it is vitally important that one knows and acknowledges the true God. When I have come to know, to experience, the graciousness of God, I will not only readily discern but firmly reject anything and everything that would temper or cloud this graciousness. This asks of me that I dare to acknowledge my God of infinite love and mercy and forgiveness. All of us know how a remark may influence one profoundly. I recall being so stirred by an observation of C.H. Dodd in his classic commentary on Romans.[2] It is particularly apt in the setting of the present book as it sets off, starkly, one image of God against another: 'The author of Hebrews has said, 'It is an awful thing to fall into the hands of the living God.' Paul, with a finer instinct, has seen that the realy awful thing is to fall out of his hands.' I grow more sure of the wisdom of that remark. The comfort is that, once within the shelter of God's hands, it is not at all easy to fall out of them. But, one must recognize the shelter.

Human Ungraciousness
There seems to be a rooted human reluctance to acknowledge and wholeheartedly welcome a gracious God – in particular when that graciousness is directed at others. One does not have to search too far for biblical instances.

1. RELUCTANT PROPHET
Despite the glowing promise of Second Isaiah (Isaiah 40-55),

2. *The Epistle of Paul to the Romans* (London: Collins, 1959), p. 55.

return from the Babylonian Exile was on a depressingly modest scale. In the tiny sixth-century Jewish state the struggle to preserve national identity was painful. It is understandable that, among the returned exiles and their descendants, in view of all they had been through and were still suffering, a certain exclusiveness, a ghetto-mentality, should have emerged – at least in some circles. Those who shared this outlook wished to cut themselves off from contact with other peoples and looked with impatience for the vengeance of God on the Gentiles. Jonah is a criticism of this stance and a bold declaration that God is God of all peoples. It is a sophisticated writing, a brilliant satire.

With splendid artistry the author contrasts the narrow, unforgiving disposition of the Israelite prophet with the open and sympathetic stance of the other actors in his story – all Gentiles. The pagan sailors were shocked to learn that anyone could bring oneself to disobey a divine command (1:10). The king of Nineveh and his people at once hearkened to the word of the prophet and converted (3:6-9). The irony is heavy: the preaching of a reluctant Jonah met with immediate and universal response in the pagan city, whereas the great prophets had, over the centuries, preached to the deaf ears of the Chosen People!

God emerges as very much the Hebrew God: he can change his mind if and when he chooses. 'When God saw what they did, how they turned from their evil ways, God changed his mind about the calamity that he had said he would bring upon them; and he did not do it' (3:10). As for Jonah: 'But this was very displeasing to Jonah, and he became angry' (4:1) He vented his anger in prayer – in complaint to God about God:

> O Lord! is not this what I said while I was still in my own country? This is why I fled do Tarshish at the beginning, for I know that you are a gracious God and merciful, slow to anger and abounding in steadfast love, and ready to

relent from punishing (4:2).

Jonah fears God. He cannot bring himself to acknowledge a God who is wholly merciful and gracious to all, a God who abounds in steadfast love of *all*. Jonah fled this gracious God. Jonah does not stand alone. There are many, far to many, who fear this disconcerting God. They are more at ease with a 'just' God, a God who goes by the book. One knows where one stands with such a God. That civilized God harbours no nasty surprises. He knows who his friends are (see Luke 18:9-14). Too often his 'friends' are in authority positions or in situations of pastoral care and make life miserable for others.

2. THE BEGRUDGER

In our reading of the parable of The Prodigal Son – The Lost Boy, if one prefers – the elder son of the story gets short shrift (Lk 15:11-32). This is unfortunate because he is, indeed, the focus of the story. The first part of this little drama portrays God's gracious forgiveness: 'I will go to my father' – nothing more is needed. The father had taken over. The sinner was warmly welcomed and reinstated without condition. It is a moment to be savoured and celebrated. The other son, the righteous, was scandalized and hurt. It is not fair! There is just his error: he had not understood that God is not fair! God is wholly merciful, boundless in his forgiveness. 'Justice' does not enter into it. The Father who had embraced the sinner is gentle, too, with the aggrieved righteous one. 'Son, you are always with me, and all that is mine is yours.'

He is in no sense worse off because God is merciful. What is in question is recognition of a merciful God. And this recognition has to be painfully practical. The elder son had washed his hands of his brother. The unwelcome and unwelcomed homecomer was 'this son of yours!' He is, by his father, delicately but unmistakedly, put right: the homecomer is 'this brother of yours.' And he was invited to enter into the celebration: 'We had to celebrate and rejoice.' The ending of the story offers a classic example of the literary feature of unresolved conflict. Its purpose is to involve the reader or hearer. We are made to wonder how we might act in the place of the elder brother. Will I stay outside, sulking? Will I welcome my sister or brother and share the joy of our Father? In effect, *I* must write the ending of this story. My ending will depend on my understanding of God – my image of God.

3. NOT AMONG YOU

Ungraciousness is not only in individual conduct. It can be on a wider scale. And it can pose as virtue rather than be seen for what it really is. 'You know that among the Gentiles those whom they recognize as their rulers lord it over them, and their great ones are tyrants over them. But it is not so among you' (Mk 10:42-43). Why is it that this word of the Lord has been, consistently, ignored? Why is it that institutionalized religion has, consistently, presented a stern image of God, has stressed the demands of God?

The reason is not far to seek. Such a God serves, very neatly, religion so structured. That demand of Jesus is an embarrassment. It is better ignored. Organized religion – despite ritual disclaimers – is much concerned with power and control. Humanly speaking, it is practically inevitable that this should be. The system takes on a life of its own and becomes obsessively protectivce of itself. It assumes a God-given status. It is upholder of God's law. It enjoys privileged insight into the mind of God. That insight is all the more convincing when 'God' is, largely, a construct of the system. In short, the system knows God and his ways. The proper role of the 'the faithful' is unquestioning obedience.

Who can, honestly, deny that such has been, traditionally, the dominant stance of the Christian Churches? 'Blind obedience' has, rightly, been castigated as refuge of perpetrators of Nazi and other atrocities. Yet, blind obedience has long been a 'virtue' fostered within the Christian Church.[3] How, in the name of God, could this have happened?. In the name of God! Not the God of Paul or of Jesus. The 'blind obedience' that the true God demands is the riddle of Job, the agony of Gethsemane. It is not a servile response to 'divine law'. It is far more radical. It is saying 'Yes' to God in face of total contradiction. It is clinging to God where such clinging seems pointless. It is letting God have the last word.

This is not to say that there is no place for institutionalized religion. What needs to be clearly understood is that a religious system, any religious system, is a human construct. As such it is always open to criticism – in particular to self-criticism: *Ecclesia semper purificanda*.[4] Vatican II, with typical candour, had the decency to acknowledge a flawed church. One can forgive a certain reluctance to embrace the *ecclesia semper reformanda* of the Reformers. The difference in formulation is not significant. More importantly, the *semper purificanda* is a healthy and welcome retreat from unrealistic triumphalism.[5]

Jesus of Nazareth was a radical critic of both the popular religion and the official Temple-religion of his day. Chapter

3. I am a religious, with a vow of obedience. My obedience is not, and cannot be, 'blind' obedience. Paradoxically, my vow of obedience is an exercise of my freedom. I freely entrust myself to the mercy of this Dominican Order. As a human being, free child of God, I have no right to abdicate my freedom (though my freedom may be taken from me – and that is the most obscene sin of all). My God does not demand blind obedience!

4. *Lumen Gentium.* chapter 1, n. 8.

5. Edward Schillebeeckx has observed: 'I recall a splendid interpretation by Thomas Aquinas of what the "rule of Christ" involves. He writes: "The power and rule of Christ over human beings is exercised by truth, justice and above all love." [*Christi potestas et imperium in homines exercetur per veritatem, per iustitiam, maxime per caritatem*' III Sent. d. 13,q.2] ... Where the church of Christ lays claim to another rule, it does not simply depart from the spirit of freedom, the Spirit of Jesus Christ, but it also fails in its duty towards the world, namely to proclaim and practise the liberating power of the Christian message credibly and understandably.' (*Church. The Human Story of God*, London: SCM Press, 1990, p. 222)

7 of Mark documents his repudiation of the 'tradition of the elders', the *halakah*. This was part of his ongoing skirmish with the Pharisees. He and they – and they were, in the main, sincerely religious people – had serious theological differences. He and they had much common ground, and so could dialogue. More than once Jesus was guest at a meal hosted by Pharisees. Jesus' sharp critique of the Temple was another matter. Here he touched a raw nerve. Together with the land of Israel, and more importantly, Torah and Temple were the pillars of Judaism. For the priesthood – effectively the religious authority – criticism of the Temple was grave indeed.

It is noteworthy that, however garbled, the charge that Jesus had sought to 'destroy' the temple figures in all passion narratives. Luke tells us (Acts 7) that his critique of the Temple sealed Stephen's fate. Jesus' critique of the Temple-system – of religion – was, historically, a factor, if not indeed, the factor, in sealing his fate. It is hazardous to challenge entrenched religion. The story of the prophets of Israel and of Christendom shows how costly. Nevertheless, the challenge is vital and must be mounted. One hopes that it is here a challenge, even if couched in admittedly timid fashion. I have no great yearning to be a martyr!

Jesus of Nazareth

Here enters the great enigma. We Christians cannot ever ignore Jesus, though we have been brilliant in denying him.

Jesus of Nazareth is, embarrassingly, a challenge to our Christology. He is also, a challenge to our theology and our ecclesiology. One comes to the riddle of Christianity. Christianity is, or ought to be, a wondrously optimistic religion. And so it is, for those who understand it. There has been much focus on the cross – and rightly so. The Christian will always remember, however, that Easter Sunday stands beyond Good Friday. The Stations of the Cross do not end at the tomb. Our faith is Easter faith.

The scandal of Jesus' death remains. Paul had to wrestle with it. He has a name for divine logic: *foolishness*. If, as a Jew, he had to struggle, painfully, with the obduracy of Israel he had, again as a Jew, earlier come to terms with a deeper problem – that of a crucified Messiah. In Galatians he declared: 'Christ redeemed us from the curse of the law by becoming a curse for us – for it is written, 'Cursed be everyone who hangs on a tree" (3:13). There he adverts to what, for any Jew, would seem to be a fatal rebuttal of the Christian claim that Jesus was Messiah. There was the contrary evidence of Torah, the unambiguous word of Deuteronomy 21:22-23 – 'When someone is convicted of a crime punishable by death and is executed, and you hang him on a tree, his corpse must not remain all night upon the tree; you shall bury him that same day, for anyone hung on a tree is under God's curse.'

In Christian tradition Jesus had been duly condemned to death by the high priest and the sanhedrin as a 'blasphemer' (Mk 14:63-64 parr.). And he had been 'hung on a tree' – crucified. Manifestly abandoned by God, he could not, by any logic, be God's Anointed One. It is evident that Paul who had, consequently, been 'a persecutor of the church' (Phil 3:6; see Gal 1:14,23) in face of the outrageous Christian claim, had had, himself, to come to terms with the 'scandal.'[6]

Paul, then, was acutely conscious of the formidable difficulty at the heart of the Christian message. If, at Caesarea Philippi, the reaction of Peter to the very suggestion that the Messiah might suffer and die was indignant denial (Mark 8:31-33) how much more unacceptable for any Jew to acknowledge as Messiah one whom God abandoned to a shameful death. As for the non-Jew: it was asking too much

6. '[Gal 3:13] "becomes a curse on our behalf": Paul envisions a divine interchange: Christ assumes humanity's situation so that humanity can assume his situation ... In other words, Paul argues that the Messiah came to redeem his own people from the curse of the Law.' (F. J. Matera, *Galatians*, Collegeville MN: Liturgical Press 1992, pp. 120, 124)

to recognize a saviour in that helpless victim on a cross. When Paul declared: 'We preach Christ crucified, a stumbling-block to Jews and folly to Gentiles' (1 Cor 1:23), he spoke from wry experience. He thought not only of the missionary challenge but, surely, recalled his personal conflict. He will not compromise. He wanted to know nothing 'except Jesus Christ and him crucified' (2:2) because it was just here he had come to discern the power and the wisdom of God (see 1:24). Nor does Paul view the resurrection of Jesus as a 'saving operation;' he would regard the resurrection as inherent in the Cross.

The resurrection showed up the Cross in its true light and demonstrated that 'God's foolishness is wiser than human wisdom, and God's weakness is stronger than human strength' (1:25). Paul would not draw a veil over the scandal of the Cross. Paul would not argue with the foolishness of God. And God's 'foolishness' was most manifest in his victory over death.

Death

Death has been swallowed up in victory.
Where, O death, is your victory?
Where, O death, is your sting? (1 Cor 15:54).

Death is the inevitable close of human life on earth. Death is passage from this world of time and space to the eternal world. Death brings encounter with God. It is the moment of truth. If one's image of God is decisive for the manner in which one lives one's life, it is crucial in determining how one faces the prospect of death. Death may come in many ways. It may be sudden and painless. It may come at the close of prolonged and painful illness. It may be the result of human cruelty. It is salutary, and comforting, to keep in mind that anguished cry of Godforsakenness: 'My God, my God, why have you abandoned me?' It is wise to recall the prayer of Gethsemane: 'If it be possible, let this cup pass from me.' Jesus did not welcome a cruel death; he shuddered at the prospect. He found, in earnest prayer to the Father, the courage to face it. Yet, shattered by the seemingly hopeless failure of his task, and in physical agony, he felt the absence of God. His prayer, wrenched from him, was lament – a cry to One who could deliver him from suffering. When one is in great pain it is not easy to pray. It is more natural to cry out. That is the pattern of Old Testament lament. That was the way of a crucified Jesus. 'My God:' that absent God was still his God. Jesus learned that God had not abandoned him.

More and more one comes to appreciate why Paul had reached the firm intent to preach the message of the cross: 'I decided to know nothing among you except Jesus Christ and him crucified' (1 Cor 2:2). The death of Jesus is our assurance that God is not aloof from human death, as he is not absent from any aspect of human life – of life, in short.

The death of Jesus, marked by an anguished cry, met a Father's response of welcome. It is humanly understandable that our human imagining should set death in a context of judgment. It is, indeed, the moment of truth. The point is, it is God's truth, not ours. That brilliant judgment-scene in Revelation says it all (see Rev 20:11-15) with its 'books' and 'the book of life.' The resurrected dead 'were judged according to their works, as recorded in the books.' That would seem to be it, then. If this were all, we have justification by works! Happily, there is that 'book of life.' Salvation is of God alone (as it was for Jesus). God has the last word. His book is book of life.

Our God has created us as free beings. He respects our freedom wholly; that is why his grace is, so often, thoroughly disguised. We come, later, to discern his graciousness in our most painful episodes. Freedom is costly; it exacts the price of responsibility. We are responsible for our deeds and our omissions. Yet, all the while, our salvation is wholly grace. 'Whoever does not receive the kingdom of God like a child shall not enter it' (Mk 10:15). 'Justified by his grace as a gift, through the redemption which is in Christ Jesus' (Rom 3:24). John the author of Revelation, like the Bible in general, does not attempt to resolve the tension. Later theologians courageously, stubbornly – and vainly – strove to find a way past the dilemma. The theologians of the Bible, in their wisdom, were content to leave the matter in the hands of God. And there is where we are: now – and we may firmly hope – where we shall be for ever.

Appendix

Chapter One has presented the phenomenon of abrupt fluctuation of judgment and salvation throughout the prophetic literature. Because I consider the matter to be so important, I supply here a list of the occurrences. The list serves a twofold purpose. Firstly, it graphically demonstrates the pervasiveness of this remarkable contrast. Then, the precise references enable the reader to check for oneself.

We are fully aware that the prophetical books are, on the whole, rather haphazard collections of prophetic oracles. This fact is of importance in our interpretation of them. Still, we are faced with the final form of each text. We may not ignore this factor. So, for instance, we need to understand why an editor felt the need to append 9:11-15 to Hosea. Surely, it was to bring it into line with the other prophetical books. I follow, then, the 'canonical' shape of the texts.

In the list, references in bold type indicate the positive word. In the main, each will follow a negative text. Where the bold type reference stands by itself it is to be set against a broader negative context.

AMOS

1:1 - 9:10	**9:11-15**

HOSEA

1:2-9;	**1:10-2:1 [Heb. 2:16-25]**
2:2-13 [Heb. 2:4-17]	**2:14-23 [Heb. 2:16-25]**
Chapters 3-10	**11:1-9**
13:12-16	**14:1-8**

ISAIAH 1–39

1:2-15	**1:16-18**
1:21-25a	**1:25b-26**

	2:2-5; 2:6-4:1; 4:2-6
7:1-13	**7:14-16**
8:16-22	**9:1-7 [Heb. 8:23-9:6]**
10:5-11	**10:20-27**
10:27b-34	**11:1-9, 10-16; 12:1-6**
24:1-22	**24:23; 25:1-10; 26:1-15; 27:12-13**
28:1-15	**28:16-17a**
29:1-16	**29:17-21**
30:1-17	**30:18-26**
32:9-14	**32:15-20; chapter 33; chapter 35**

SECOND ISAIAH (40-55)

The 'Book of Consolation,' with its message of exuberant hope, stands out against the traumatic experience of national disaster and Exile. Here, more than elsewhere, the relevant texts appear apart from an immediately contiguous contrast.

	40:1-11.27-31.
	41:8-16.17-20.
	The Servant Songs: **42:1-7; 49:1-7**
	50:4-9; 52:13-53:12.
42:18-25	**43:1-7, 16-21.**
43:22-28	**44:1-8.**
44:9-20	**44:21-28.**
45:9-13	**45:14-17.**
	45:20-25 – universal salvation.
	46:3-4.12-13 – combination.
48:1-8	**48:9-11.17-21.**
	49:8-13.
	49:14-26
50:1-3	**51:1-8**
	51:9-23 – infidelity/salvation
	52:1-2.3-6.7-12
	54:1-5
	54:4-10 – brief abandonment/love
	54:11-17
	55:1-13

THIRD ISAIAH (56-66)

	56:1-8 – universal salvation
56:9 - 57:13;	**57:14-21**
58:1-5	**58:6-14**
59:1-19	**59:20-21**
	Chapters 60 to 62
65:1-7	**65:8-10**
65:11-16	**65:17-25**

66:1-5	**66:10-13**
66:14-16	**66:18-23** – universal salvation

MICAH

1:1-2:11	**2:12-13**
3:1-12	**4:1-8**
4:9-12	**4:13-5:1**
	4:2-5a [Heb. 5:1-4a]
7:8-10	**7:11-20.**

ZEPHANIAH

3:1-11	**3:12-20**

HABAKKUK

Chapter 3 (3:17-19)

JEREMIAH

3:6-10	**3:11-13.15-18**
3:19-25	**4:1-2**
16:1-13	**16:14-15**
23:1-2	**23:3-8**
25:8-11	**25:12-14**
29:4-9	**29:10-14**
	30:1-31:28 – restoration of Israel
30:12-15	**30:16-17**
	31:31-34 – new covenant/new people
	31:35-37
32:26-35	**32:36-44**
33:5	**33:6-9**
	33:14-16
	33:19-22, 23-26
	50:4-10
50:17	**50:18-20**
	50:33-34

EZEKIEL

11:1-12	**11:14-20**
16:1-52	**16:53-63**
17:11-21	**17:22-24**
20:1-39	**20:40-44**
	28:24-26
	33:10-11
34:7-10	**34:11-16, 23-31**
36:16-21	**36:22-36**
	37:1-14, 15-28

39:21-29
Chapters 40-48 – restoration

ZECHARIAH

1:7-12	**1:13-17**
1:18-21	**2:1-13**
7:8-14	**8:1-8, 9-13, 14-17**
	8:20-23 – universalism
	9:9-17
	10:6-12
	12:1-9
	14:1-11

MALACHI

3:13-15	**3:16-18**
	4:5-6 [Heb 3:2-24]

JOEL

2:1-11	**2:12-18**
	2:23-29 [Heb. **2:23-3:2**]
	3:1, 18-21 [Heb. **4:1, 18-21**]

OBADIAH

Vv 15-21